SHADOWS OF TREBLINKA

Shadows of Treblinka

MIRIAM KUPERHAND

and

SAUL KUPERHAND

Introduction by Alan Adelson

UNIVERSITY OF ILLINOIS PRESS

URBANA AND CHICAGO

Publication of this book was supported by
the Sheldon Drobny Family Endowment
for the University of Illinois Press

Library of Congress Cataloging-in-Publication Data
Kuperhand, Miriam, 1926–
Shadows of Treblinka / Miriam Kuperhand and
Saul Kuperhand ; introduction by Alan Adelson.
p.   cm.
Includes bibliographical references (p.   ) and index.
ISBN 0-252-02339-0 (acid-free paper)
1. Jews—Persecutions—Poland—Kaluszyn (Warsaw).
2. Holocaust, Jewish (1939–1945)—Poland—Kaluszyn
(Warsaw)—Personal narratives. 3. Kuperhand, Miriam, 1926–   .
4. Kuperhand, Saul, 1922–   . 5. Treblinka (Concentration camp).
6. World War, 1939–1945—Jewish resistance—Poland.
7. Kaluszyn (Warsaw, Poland)—Ethnic relations.
I. Kuperhand, Saul, 1922–   . II. Title.
DS135.P62K31845   1998
940.53'18'094384—ddc21   98-8890
CIP

CONTENTS

Long Days, Dark Nights

BY MIRIAM KUPERHAND

Escape from Treblinka

BY SAUL KUPERHAND

MAP AND ILLUSTRATIONS FOLLOW PAGE *84*

Of Love and Anger—Two Accounts of Survival

ALAN ADELSON

Holocaust memoirs are literary survivors. Those few that emerge from the dark silence that characterizes the postwar lives of most Jewish survivors reach the printed page against terrible odds, for their authors must meet arduous editorial demands even as they fight the desire to put the horrors they have known behind them and to focus instead for a sustained period—in the case of the Kuperhands, six years—on searching out and compiling suppressed memories.

Miriam and Saul Kuperhand were both retired from their family clothing business, living in a duplex home in the Canarsie section of Brooklyn, New York, when Miriam, at age sixty-five, began to write down in her adopted English language her recollections of those harrowing adolescent years that would become "Long Days, Dark Nights." To keep her husband from interrupting her, she sat him down and told him, "Write your story too, Saul, and when I'm done, I'll help you." He wrote "Escape from Treblinka" in Yiddish; she later translated it into English, questioning him all the while, pressing for details and continuity until she had helped him flesh out his far more painful story. Their notebooks were then passed on to Isaac Mozeson, whose additional inquiries brought fuller detail to both memoirs and, through carefully collaborative revision, added his writer's gift of language. After several drafts, and bolstered by the annotations of Daniel Soyer, a professor of history at Fordham University, the text was finally ready for publication.

Shadows of Treblinka stands as a fundamental challenge to anyone who would assert that only those who were murdered fully experienced the Holocaust. Indeed, after not only witnessing but eluding the juggernaut to exterminate the Jews, these two innocents have lived on for five decades with their terrible and real knowledge of humankind's most brutal and evil side. It was the need to share the burden of that understanding that prompted the Kuperhands to write this book. As Miriam Kuperhand puts it: "The more I learned about Nazi thoroughness, the more I began to see my survival as a miracle. I must have survived for a reason, and that is why I must testify about what happened."

The Kuperhands' accounts will startle some historians of the Holocaust. They reveal that well before many Jews in the authors' community of Siemiatycze boarded the trains that brought them to Treblinka to die they apparently knew of the productivity in death being achieved at the now-notorious facility some forty miles away.

This two-part memoir counters the often-held belief that all the Jews of Europe went like sheep to the trains when the Germans ordered them to do so. The Jewish populations of countless communities did typically file in an orderly fashion into the cattle cars. From the photographs, films, and military records that remain, we know that relatively few troops or police were needed to keep them in line. Many Jews were deceived or were ignorant of the fate intended for them, while others either had no recourse or saw insufficient threat to justify the deadly risk of resistance. But for the Kuperhands—and certainly for others—their knowledge of the mass murder that the Germans were perpetrating was undeniable, and submission to the Nazi-organized genocide was for them instinctually impossible.

In *Shadows of Treblinka* we find vivid accounts of individual and family resistance—of Miriam's family hiding in an underground bunker to avoid deportation, then living under subhuman conditions in the wartorn Polish countryside, in constant jeopardy of betrayal and sudden death; and of Saul fleeing from a death camp that absolutely no one was supposed to survive and bear witness to. The Kuperhands' defiance of the Germans is only as remarkable as their courage and discipline in recollecting these horrors and offering them in this book to chasten humankind. Yet embedded without fanfare in the Kuperhands' narratives are those momentous acts that enabled them to get out of the genocidal rapids, graphically determining impulses that sprang from their autonomous instincts to survive.

Half a century after the Germans were stopped just short of their goal of completely annihilating European Jewry, historians continue to search for strands of documentation pertaining to what the Jews knew about the genocidal process while it was taking place. Diaries, chronicles, and documents have not resolved many basic questions related to what the Jews knew and whether or not that knowledge encouraged resistance. The 6.5 million dead cannot speak for themselves, and contemporaneous documentation is all too rare. Correspondence among Jews during the period was extremely limited and was almost certain to have been reviewed, if not dictated, by the Germans. The very few diaries and chronicles that have survived provide a precious and immediate view of the desperate months and years of Jewish life in bondage to the German destroyers.

Logic certainly suggests that despite their relative helplessness, concentrated as they were in slave camps without arms, many more Jews would have attempted to fight against boarding the trains if they knew the fate that awaited them. So in the absence of broad evidence revealing more precisely what many Jews knew and expected during the period, the rarity of resistance has commonly been held to prove that the Germans succeeded in keeping the existence of the death camps secret from the Jews. Yet the eminent Holocaust historian Raul Hilberg and others have repeatedly highlighted indications that contradict these assumptions of Jewish ignorance, stressing that even in the supposedly sealed ghettos there was awareness of the genocide. Written in the notorious Łódź Ghetto, an urban slave camp that is typically considered by historians as having been kept "hermetically sealed" by the Germans, Dawid Sierakowiak's diary suggests he somehow obtained precise knowledge of when the extermination of Jews was halted in the distant village of Chelmno by the Rollkommando, the mobile killing unit that had taken tens of thousands of Jews out of the ghetto.*

* See Dawid Sierakowiak, *The Diary of Dawid Sierakowiak,* ed. Alan Adelson (New York: Oxford University Press, 1996), 240.

There is much in *Shadows of Treblinka* that supports this analysis. The Kuperhands make it clear that rumors abounded for months of mass killings in gas chambers before the Siemiatycze Jews were sent off. Miriam's family was in a position to act on the knowledge: "Rumors flew concerning large-scale deportations [to the gas chambers], and we knew our family could not risk another selection," she writes. "Father discussed the situation with us, and we agreed to build a bunker in our backyard where we could hide during future roundups by the Nazis. We knew that if our underground bunker were to be discovered it would mean certain execution, but we decided that we had no choice." They proceeded to dig the bunker, complete with a meter-deep tunnel to the winter potato store, and connected one end of it to the town's sewer system. "[We] knew where to go the moment the end seemed near. We did not know if we would be safe, even temporarily, but we would not go on that mass transport to Treblinka."

Saul Kuperhand writes: "Dark rumors swept through the ghetto like fallen leaves, rumors that Jews who could not work would not even rate the ghetto's slow murder from starvation and disease. The ghettos of neighboring towns were being liquidated one by one. What was happening to all the Jews? They were being taken in cattle cars to a facility called Treblinka. We envisioned a forced labor camp, another era of slavery akin to what the Jews had experienced in ancient Egypt." Later he declares: "The rumors of deportation to the Treblinka death camp were confirmed by information bought from two German officers. The news flew everywhere. The Jews of Siemiatycze were in a panic. Where could we hide? What should we do? From where would our salvation come?"

Like most working-class Jews, Saul Kuperhand's family had no means by which to save themselves. In the end they were forced to board the trains that would carry them to a facility at Treblinka that eventually devoured more than 800,000 Jews and Gypsies, including almost the entire Jewish population of Warsaw—some 450,000 people, which at the time was the largest concentration of Jews in the world.

What set Miriam and Saul Kuperhand apart from the vast majority of European Jews and enabled them to live? Why did they—and in Miriam's case, her entire family—manage to break out of the Nazis' well-organized grasp? As pious Orthodox Jews, both authors offer the belief that their fates were determined according to God's will. Miriam

Kuperhand writes that "all this must have been part of G-d's plan to keep [the family] alive. We never know the reason for the suffering, but the faithful can believe that it is all for our ultimate good." She also recalls, "I could not understand G-d's plan in all of this, but I did pray to Him to preserve my life and that of my brother." (In strict observance of the commandment not to take the Lord's name in vain, Orthodox Jews adopted the practice of not even spelling out the word, so it appears throughout the text as G-d.)

Miriam and Saul Kuperhand both fled from the Nazi-organized genocide and were then forced to live for years more or less at the mercy of Polish farm families. For this reason, *Shadows of Treblinka* is also a wonderful source of information on the still-delicate issue of how Polish Christians related to the destruction of the country's Jewish citizens. It also conveys rich insight into how surviving Jewish victims of the Holocaust look upon the treatment they received from their Polish neighbors before, during, and after the war.

In "Escape from Treblinka" we are offered numerous glimpses of the intense climate of persecution that was building up against the Jews of Poland well before the German invasion of September 1939. As a tough Jewish youth, Saul Kuperhand stood up to the Polish "thugs" who made a practice of broadcasting their hateful slogans and of randomly beating and stabbing Jews. He recounts an incident during which the community's vigilant young Jews summoned scores of their own to confront such hooligans outside a restaurant. Many of the Poles were badly beaten, and a number of Jewish youths were arrested as a result. The author is clearly proud to have been among those able "to stifle their Polish slogans of hate." He writes: "These dark rumblings should have given us adequate warning, but everyone thought the storm would pass us by."

In "Long Days, Dark Nights," Miriam Kuperhand describes how Zionist youth organizations offered a way to support self-respect and hope among the young Jewish population even as they experienced increasing discrimination and persecution: "Zionism gave us second-class Polish citizens new pride in our Jewish identity. . . . I was caught up in the Zionist wave and looked forward to emigrating to a place where the people would be as warm as the climate. In Palestine every stone I moved, every tree I planted would link me to a long, glorious past and to a bright new future for my people."

Within this continuum of ethnic strife, the book describes many local Poles welcoming the Germans, including some who avidly enlisted in the Nazi program of confiscating Jewish property, even voluntarily exterminating Jews. Miriam Kuperhand writes: "As we slunk back to our homes we could hardly believe the behavior of many of our Polish neighbors. They hugged and kissed the German soldiers as though they were liberators instead of murderous invaders. Polish girls presented the Nazis with bouquets of flowers and marched arm in arm with them."

While acknowledging the bravery and righteousness of a family of Polish Catholics who hid and fed her own family during the war at the risk of instant execution if they were caught, she bitterly condemns their people for participating in the extermination of Poland's Jews. "For every noble Pole who risked all to rescue a fellow human being," she writes, "there were ten scoundrels who hunted Jews for a livelihood." "Jackals," she calls them. They collaborated with the Germans and seemed to delight in killing their former neighbors. "How deep was their hatred," she wonders, "for a gentle people who worked so hard and contributed so much to building up the Polish economy?. . . How could they use human remains to fertilize ground on which they grew the grain that they fed to their hogs? How could they use cherished headstones to make decorative footpaths in their yards?"

The ethical contradictions of the Holocaust, a period of pervasive moral compromise unprecedented in human history, are epitomized by the opposing views that have prevailed regarding the actions of Poland's home army, the Armia Krajowa. The AK's assistance to the Jewish leaders of the Warsaw Ghetto Uprising has been extensively documented.* Yet at least by name the Polish military organization that supported the Jews in the Warsaw Ghetto and is commonly honored for heroism in contemporary Poland is thought by many Polish-Jewish survivors to have participated in the genocide in rural areas. "While some Poles celebrated the Armia Krajowa as partisans who fought against the Nazis, the Jews knew that they were just as bad as the Ger-

---

* For an authoritative account of contact between the Jewish Fighting Organization and the Armia Krajowa, see Yitzchak Zuckerman's *A Surplus of Memory: A Chronicle of the Warsaw Ghetto Uprising* (Berkeley: University of California Press, 1992).

mans," Miriam Kuperhand states without qualification. "Just as the Nazis diverted much of their wartime resources to implementing their 'Final Solution,' these partisans often spent more energy hunting Jews than harassing the German occupiers." According to Saul Kuperhand, there was a "righteous Gentile [who] was the savior of many Jews," a duke whose barns and lands near the village of Bryki harbored many hidden Jewish refugees. But Duke Krakuwka's son "helped the Polish nationalist partisans, the Armia Krajowa[,] . . . telling these killers where they could find helpless Jews to plunder and murder. Instead of coordinating activities with Jewish partisans in the woods, they would attack Jewish groups at every opportunity."

Miriam Kuperhand tells of Jews who tried to reclaim their homes or businesses after the war and met resistance from Poles. The incidents she details underscore the material basis for the Polish-Jewish conflict, particularly after the war. She recounts that a man named Benny Leff tried to take back his mill in Siemiatycze and was killed by a "bloodthirsty militia" that Jews in the area called the AK. In fact, the group might well have had no connection with the original Polish home army, which was formally dissolved in 1939; however, it is well established that bands of AK soldiers *did* remain together and often linked up with partisan units to fight against the Germans in the same heavily forested areas and swamplands into which fugitive Jews fled. Chance contacts between the groups were frequent and unpredictable.*

The authors' sweeping judgments, such as Miriam Kuperhand's declaration that "our saviors [the Lescynskys] were the righteous exceptions that proved the unfortunate rule" and Saul's emphatic statement that "all the Germans and Poles, with a few glorious exceptions, were the enemy," will no doubt cause pain for many Poles who today argue for recognition of those among them who did nothing to assist the genocide, and of those who risked their lives to protect Jews and now express bereavement at the loss of them from their culture.

Few people can know better than the Kuperhands how legitimate such calls for differentiation are. Half a century later these two groups are only beginning to reconsider one another. In the course of such rapprochement, close attention to the actual circumstances that were

---

* For a highly detailed account of a Jewish partisan's fugitive life in the Polish wilds, see Shalom Yoran's memoir *The Defiant* (New York: St. Martin's Press, 1996).

experienced during those deadly years by both Polish and Jewish families is possible. At Yad Vashem, the Holocaust memorial in Israel, "Righteous Gentiles" who protected Jews are recognized and honored in a garden that bears their names. One can only hope that Holocaust awareness and scholarship—two distinct processes—will prevent the truly heroic examples of families who risked their lives to act humanely and conscientiously from being tarred over by the broad brush of intolerance and, perhaps worse, forgotten.

The interlocking memoirs of Miriam and Saul Kuperhand stand as eyewitness testimonies to the destruction of European Jewry, even as they offer readers glimpses into the unyielding will to live that hardened within the authors as the genocide of their people progressed. Quietly yet passionately, these pages offer up a bitter success story; these two narratives are as unusual as their pained authors. Of Siemiatcyze's 6,000 Jews, only 35 survived the most murderous crusade ever mounted by humankind. Two of them now share their remarkable stories with the world.

ACKNOWLEDGMENTS

This account shall be a monument to the millions of unburied, unrecorded victims of Nazi mass murder. For the crime of being born Jewish, these millions of innocent men, women, and children were uprooted and systematically exterminated. Many were transported in cattle cars to be poisoned in the gas chambers and turned into so much ash in the crematoria. Others were machine-gunned to death after being forced to march to open ditches at the outskirts of their towns. Some died more slowly of starvation and disease in the urban killing fields called ghettos; others died while in inhuman work camps. A few thousand had the privilege of dying with weapons in their hands, battling the Nazi oppressors as partisans in the forests and cities.

May this written testimony serve as a memorial candle burning in honor of all the martyrs who fell. May it serve as a record of their evaporated lives.

By the grace of G-d I have reached the age of seventy-two. It is time to speak up or remain shrouded in an awful silence. I owe it to my children, grandchildren, and surviving family finally to unburden myself of these memories.   —*Miriam Kuperhand*

Acknowledgments

I am grateful for the prodding of my wife, Miriam, and the skills of Alan Adelson of the Jewish Heritage Project in New York, Isaac Mozeson, and Daniel Soyer. Thanks to our daughter-in-law Suzanne Kuperhand for helping us put the book together. I dedicate this to my parents, Abe and Doba; my eight brothers, Yakov-Hirsh, Usher, David, Banish, Beryl, Aaron, Simche, and Yiddle; and my sister, Sarale. —*Saul Kuperhand*

Long Days, Dark Nights

MIRIAM KUPERHAND

Made in Kałuszyn

I was not born in Warsaw, Paris, or Berlin but in the small Polish town of Kałuszyn on May 10, 1926. A mostly Jewish town of about 6,000 souls, Kałuszyn had several small factories that produced woolen prayer shawls and fur coats. The town was dominated by a single large commercial street. Walking the length of Warszawska Street, one encountered the sound of weaving, the smell of leather and fur, and the sight of crowds of men and women coming out of organizational meetings.

Warszawska Street was a marketplace for a wide variety of ideas and movements. Zionist, Socialist, and Communist organizations all had their offices and meeting halls there, competing with the dozens of religious institutions for charity, learning, and worship. Among many small synagogues and yeshivas one could find the *hevra kadisha* (burial society), the *hachnasus kallah* (new brides' fund), and the religious Zionist organization. Most of the townspeople were religious Jews, but there was a small group of active Communists who would occasionally bait the police by hanging red banners on the overhead electrical wires. Nobody seemed to mind these secular messianists, and the police chases and arrests added some much-needed excitement.

Only fifty-six kilometers from Warsaw, the capital of Poland, Kałuszyn boasted a highly rated yeshiva that attracted students from far and wide. There were no dormitory facilities, so students followed the custom of boarding at the homes of volunteers. My mother was always kept busy with two extra boys from the yeshiva to care for and feed. She also cooked meals for the poor. I remember holding onto her big shawl as a girl of four or five as she delivered the meals.

When she had a chance to relax, Mother would read all kinds of books. She used to take me with her to the library to pick up or return the secular books that complemented her religious reading. She also volunteered for various synagogue committees, including the burial society, where she helped ritually prepare the bodies of deceased women for burial. Little did she know that all too soon some other woman would be performing this ultimate act of kindness for her.

Mother took ill at the age of twenty-nine and had to stay at home. Happy to have her around all day, I did not understand the seriousness of her condition. She battled tuberculosis for three years before succumbing at age thirty-two. I was only six years old at the time, my brother only ten. I was too young to fully understand how profound my loss was.

After Mother's death we were too busy to sit and mourn our tragedy for long. My brother and I had to assume responsibility for cooking, cleaning, and doing the wash. We even delivered Father's meal to him at the factory. When not at work, Father threw himself into charitable activities. On Fridays, when work ended early, he would wash, change his clothes, and make the rounds with a *pushka* (charity box) to collect money for the new brides' fund and for the burial society. Even with his own young wife in the world of the eternal Father continued to work for those who were too poor to afford proper weddings or funerals. He derived much satisfaction from his charitable efforts. Along with time, they must have served to heal his emotional wounds.

My own ill health also kept Father busy, monitoring the fever that would linger with me for weeks on end. I had developed inflammations in my kidneys and lungs, and my poor father had to bring doctors from Warsaw to diagnose and treat my condition. Medicines, bedrest, and time finally healed the sickness that must have come from my broken heart.

To comfort us in our loss, Father showered us with gifts and attention. He never refused a request for toys and often treated us to movies and the theater. On holidays he took us to visit relatives. But pampering his children was no life for a young, handsome widower who

4

made a comfortable living and showed it by dressing well. He was introduced to a friend's sister-in-law, a divorcée named Roiske, and a romance soon blossomed.

Shortly after Father and Roiske married we moved to the town of Siemiatycze.* It was 1937 and I was eleven years old. Still hurting from the loss of my mother, I found it difficult to leave my friends, my school, and my town to start all over in another place. Home provided little comfort. My stepmother often yelled at me, never satisfied with me or my contributions to the housework. I could not compete with my three-year-old stepsister, my stepmother's daughter from her previous marriage.

* Siemiatycze is located eighty-two kilometers south of Białystok on the Kamianka River, near where it flows into the Bug River. In 1921 some 3,718 Jews comprised nearly two-thirds of the population.

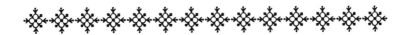

The Cemetery of Siemiatycze

The town of Siemiatycze was famous throughout Poland for a certain legend concerning its cemetery. The incredible events supposedly took place in the nineteenth century and are recorded in town annals as the truth. I'll let you decide how much of the story you want to believe.

It began when the rich and powerful Duke Jabłonowski passed away, leaving his estate to the Duchess Ana Sapieha Jabłonowska.* With the backing of the Polish king, Stanisław II, the duchess decided to establish her residence in Siemiatycze and build up the town as an important provincial capital with a substantial central marketplace.† She had a beautiful palace erected and surrounded it with finely sculptured gardens that were encircled by symmetrical orchards and groves.

Just beyond the duchess's vast and opulent estate lay the Jewish cemetery. The cries and lamentations of mourners at burial services irritated her as she strolled on her grounds, and she had plans for expansion that involved those hallowed acres. The duchess summoned the Jewish community leaders to her palace and offered various pro-

---

* The Duchess Jabłonowska lived from 1728 to 1800.

† Stanisław II (August Poniatowski, 1732–98) was the last king of Poland before the country was dismantled between 1772 and 1795.

posals. In exchange for their cemetery she would give the Jews a large new one that was closer to town. In addition, she offered to have several large commercial buildings erected on Siemiatycze's central street to house all the Jewish-run stores and businesses. Each of the structures would include residential second floors to house the families of the town's Jewish merchants and manufacturers.

On top of this the duchess offered the Jews a special dispensation to use her woods freely for much-needed fuel. This added incentive was worth many thousands of rubles to the owners of homes and businesses. But the members of the Jewish delegation shook their heads and refused to negotiate. This cemetery was where their parents, spouses, and children lay in eternal rest. Hundreds of plots were already reserved to receive the remains of additional loved ones.

The Duchess Jabłonowska would not take no for an answer. To further her plans she searched the Siemiatycze community for a Jewish man who would accept money in exchange for helping her from the inside. The turncoat's name was Kadishewitz, and he advised the duchess that only terror would part the Jews from their cemetery. The next morning the Jews discovered that scores of tombstones had been smashed and many corpses roughly exhumed.

The Jews of Siemiatycze were deeply pained and outraged. Instead of capitulating, they sent men to watch over the graves twenty-four hours a day. They raised their voices in lamentation and prayer to ask forgiveness from the departed for allowing such an atrocity to occur. The duchess sent soldiers to the cemetery to evict them, but the Jews lay down in protest, guarding the graves with their own bodies. The enraged duchess ordered her soldiers to beat up any Jew who refused to leave. The Jews suffered many casualties.

The cemetery was finally cleared of living Jews, and the work of removing tombstones and landscaping the duchess's coveted new grounds commenced. The workers met no further resistance until they came to the tomb of the community's most revered scholar and saint. As they prepared to uproot the *tsadik's* large stone using a rope and a team of horses, both men and horses suddenly dropped dead. More men were called to the task and they too were miraculously stricken.

Now it was the Poles who were terrified. The Duchess Jabłonowska turned to her Jewish advisor, Mr. Kadishewitz, who suggested overcoming the deadly curse by using men who were seventh-generation first-borns. The special crew was assembled and the work of transforming the cemetery continued without incident.

The former cemetery was split into two sections, one on either side of a wide boulevard named Aleja Legionowa. The regal street, lined with trees, flowers, and bushes, linked the duchess's palace with the surrounding villas and led to the new center of town. Wealthy aristocratic families built their mansions on this street, living on beautifully landscaped estates behind high walls.

As promised, the duchess allotted the Jews a new space on the other side of town for their cemetery. The first candidate for burial was none other than the wretched Mr. Kadishewitz, who died young, childless, and in an official state of excommunication. Although it was agreed that nobody was less deserving of a proper Jewish burial, the committee nevertheless consented to bury Mr. Kadishewitz near the cemetery gate. Somehow his body rose to the top of the grave and the next day birds and other animals were discovered feasting on the corpse.

When the Duchess Jabłonowska's first-born son died suddenly and for no apparent reason, even she was convinced that she had incurred the wrath of Heaven for her cold-hearted sins against the Jews. With anguish and fear the duchess assembled the Jewish elders and begged their forgiveness. By way of compensation she arranged for the construction of a magnificent synagogue.* The community summoned the finest architects of the time who created an ornate, oriental-style building with beautiful stained glass windows, marble floors, and pews of fine wood and brass. Elaborate handcrafted designs covered the walls and ceilings, and the most talented artists of central Europe painted murals depicting the twelve tribes of Israel and other biblical scenes.

The Jewish community of Siemiatycze only slowly accepted this lavish gift of penance. They could not forget or forgive the desecration of the graves of their sainted ancestors, but they eventually began to pray for the well-being of the duchess and her family every Sabbath in their new synagogue.

Another chapter in the legend of Siemiatycze was written during one of the duchess's regular carriage rides with a special contingent

* The synagogue was built in 1755.

of uniformed guards along the banks of the Bug River.* One day the ride was taking longer than usual and the drivers and guards began to wonder why the duchess had not yet ordered them home. They stopped the luxurious carriage, opened the doors, and saw—to their amazement—that the duchess had vanished without a trace. The guards were later found drowned in the river. It was as though the river had reached out to bury them in its waters. As word of the disaster spread like a firestorm, the townspeople observed that the guards who drowned were the very same men who had destroyed the Jewish cemetery.

The Siemiatycze synagogue again figured in the history of the region during the Polish revolt against the Russians in 1863.† As the front line neared the town, a major battle developed and the Russians overpowered the Polish militia. The duchess's palace and the town were bombarded, sending both up in flames. When the smoke cleared only one building remained—the magnificent synagogue. Its survival was nothing less than a miracle, and it still stands today.

By the time I moved to Siemiatycze in 1937, only the town's history was extraordinary. Changing circumstances had left the synagogue in disrepair. As the magnificent biblical murals began to peel, the walls were daubed with cheap paint. The congregation tried to sell off some of the antiques to raise money for repairs. Offered only 200 rubles for these treasures, the congregation decided to keep its few remaining pieces of master craftsmanship. By the time of the Nazi occupation the synagogue had only its elaborate charity box and Elijah's chair to remind the world of its former glory.

---

* The Bug River, a major tributary of the Vistula, runs for some 800 kilometers. From 1939 to 1941 it formed the border between the German and Soviet zones of occupation in Poland. After 1945 it marked Poland's frontier with the Soviet Union.

† The January Insurrection aimed to re-establish Poland's independence. Although it soon became apparent that the rebellion would fail, it was not completely suppressed until 1865. Some sections of the Jewish population actively supported the rebellion, many of whose leaders espoused liberal principles.

A Life of Fur

Siemiatycze was populated by about 6,000 Jews and a handful of Catholics. Its economy revolved around several factories and their supporting businesses. The chief industry was the production of ceramic tiles for use in heating and cooking ovens as well as in bathrooms. One ceramics factory, owned by the Belkes family, was nationally known as a major exporter of tiles. A second important factory owned by the same family produced small wooden nails and other materials needed for the manufacture of shoes. Other leading families who owned factories in town were the Daitches, the Radzinskis, the Kotlers, and the Maliniaks. Besides ceramics, Siemiatycze was known for the manufacture of bricks, wood panels, and other building materials, shipping them throughout Poland and beyond.

Most of the Jews of Siemiatycze were highly committed to secular and religious causes and organizations. The young people were fired up with the dream of returning to the land of Israel. Zionist organizations ranged from the secular Hashomer Hatzair to the right-wing Betar and on to religious groups like Bnei Akiva and Mizrachi.* *Halutzim* (pioneers) ran a farm on the outskirts of Siemiatycze where they honed

* Hashomer Hatzair (the socialist Young Guard) was established in 1916 and evolved from a scouting organization into a left-wing socialist-Zionist youth movement. It pro-

their farming skills while waiting for visas to emigrate to Palestine, a period of preparation they called *hachshara*. They hoped soon to farm their ancient homeland and to build up the Yishuv (Jewish settlement under the British mandate).*

There was no visible rancor among the Zionists, the Socialist Bundists, and the town's Jewish majority, both *misnagdim* (more sober and scholarly) and *hasidim* (more populist and mystical).† Rather than congregating in the synagogue the duchess had paid for, the Jewish community dispersed into local *shtiblach* (small synagogues) and *yeshivot* (institutes of Jewish learning). While some children attended the Polish public school, most Jewish children went to whichever private religious school fit their parents' budget. There were the tiny *hedorim* (one-room schools), where beginning at age three children received instruction from a single rabbi; the larger Talmud Torah schools for older boys; the Beit Yacov schools for girls; and the Tarbut school, which was the best and most expensive alternative to private tutors.‡

---

moted Hebrew culture and encouraged its members to join kibbutzim in Palestine. Betar (Brit Trumpeldor) formed in 1923, taking the name of the Zionist hero Yosef Trumpeldor (1880–1920). It advocated the ideas of the Revisionist Zionist leader Vladimir Jabotinsky (1880–1920), opposing socialism and calling for a Jewish state on both sides of the Jordan River. Founded in 1902, the Mizrachi movement aimed to combine Orthodox Judaism with Zionism. (Its name, which means "Eastern" in Hebrew, was originally an acronym for *merkaz ruhani*, or "spiritual center.") Bnei Akiva (Sons of Akiva) was the youth movement of the labor wing of Mizrachi. It took its name from the Talmudic sage who lived in the first and second centuries C.E. Akiva supported the Bar Kokhba revolt against Roman rule in Palestine (132–35 C.E.) and was executed by Roman authorities for defying their ban on the teaching of Torah.

* Hehalutz (the Pioneers), which maintained a number of training camps in Poland to prepare young people for agricultural work in Palestine, claimed 41,000 members in 1933.

† The Bund (General Jewish Workers' Alliance) was founded in Vilna in 1897. Secular in outlook, it advocated socialism, supported Yiddish culture, and opposed Zionism. By the end of the 1930s it was the most popular Jewish party in Poland. Hasidism was characterized by ecstatic prayer and by its followers' devotion to charismatic religious leaders who established their courts in a number of towns. At first quite violent, the conflict between *hasidim* and *misnagdim* subsided by the early nineteenth century when the two groups realized they faced a common enemy in the growing secularization of Jewish life.

‡ Supported by the Orthodox Agudat Israel party, the Beit Yacov (Beth Jacob) girls' schools combined traditional Judaism with modern educational methods. The first Beit Yacov school was established in Krakow in 1917; by 1929 there were 147 such schools in Poland. Tarbut schools, which offered a pro-Zionist Hebrew education, numbered more than 200 in Poland. The Tarbut school in Siemiatycze was known as the Kadimah Hebrew Public School (*kadimah* means "forward").

Tarbut means "culture" in Hebrew, and the Tarbut school in Siemia-tycze was a product of the town's monied intelligentsia. It featured a demanding curriculum of both secular and religious studies, taught in both Polish and Hebrew. Graduates of this school were well equipped for any Polish gymnasium and for the pursuit of higher education at the university. The school's principal, Yehudah Kohut, fit my youthful ideal of a refined scholar. It still disturbs me to think of this modest, highly educated, and personable man perishing in the Treblinka gas chambers with the rest of his family.

In Siemiatycze we lived in a private house with Father's fur factory on the premises. He had become an expert in the field by working for many years with the Berman family of furriers in Kałuszyn. Twice a year Father made long trips to Kołomyja and to Leipzig, Germany, to pur-chase raw pelts for his business. His specialty was treating lamb's wool for use in trimming top-of-the-line overcoats. The most treacherous part of his work was mixing all sorts of chemicals to treat and dye the skins. Even a slight miscalculation could ruin the materials.

From all that smelly hard work came beautiful leather, fur, and sheepskin coats in many different colors and styles, some with elabo-rate designs and patterns. Father even made use of the small leftover pieces, turning them into hats and gloves. He provided local farmers with sheepskin coats, charging them only for labor and other materi-als if they supplied the sheared fleece. He also got along well with his employees and customers. The successful enterprise added some much-needed stability to our lives.

In time I got used to new friends and began to love my new school. My health was not quite 100 percent, but I improved with each regu-larly scheduled doctor's checkup. I now wanted to get better; besides, I needed strength for the cooking, cleaning, washing, and gardening I had to do after returning home from school.

Laundry in the 1930s was no easy matter. I first had to draw water from the neighbor's well and carry it home in two heavy buckets on a long pole balanced across my shoulders. Laundering required even more trips to the well than did watering the lawn, and it also meant heating the water on the stove. To get the stove started I had to lug coal up from the cellar and bring firewood in from the backyard. If the wood was not sufficiently dry, I practically had to blow my lungs out to get the fire going. After the water was heated I poured it into a huge barrel and let the laundry soak in detergent overnight. The next day meant lots of work with the scrubbing board. Then the scrubbed laundry had to be boiled on the stove and rinsed out, after which I would begin the work of bleaching and starching. No typical twelve-year-old girl looked forward to doing the laundry.

All that housework made it hard for me to get my homework done, and I found that hiding from my stepmother each night was the only solution. My best hiding places were in Father's factory complex. In the evening I could always find a deserted area in which to work undisturbed—once I got used to the strong chemical and leather smells, that is.

My brother was spared the curse of housework, but I can't say he got off easy. He worked very hard with my father in the furrier's workshop, lugging heavy materials, mixing strong chemicals, and finishing both sides of every skin that went into a coat or accessory. Since he worked so hard during the day, my parents expected him to go out and enjoy himself in the evening. He often went downtown to meet his friends. They were a nice bunch of boys and girls from fine families and never attracted negative attention. I have tried to maintain contact with the people in his crowd. Sadly, very few of them survived the Holocaust.

My own social life was more limited, but I did manage to have one. Sometimes I had to sneak out of the house to see my friends. I might receive a lecture or be punished in some way for doing so, but I never let the consequences stop me. I mostly got together with girlfriends from school. We would talk about writers and books we had read, enthusiastically exchanging opinions and recommendations. I must admit that not all our little meetings were so cultured. We also talked about boys we knew and shared all the latest gossip.

How exciting it was when one of my girlfriends acquired a gramophone! Singing along with the scratchy music and dancing to the tunes thrilled us. We also talked about our plans for the future. We all dreamed of doing different things when we got older and finished school. Some girls thought only of whom they would marry, while others longed for professional fulfillment as well. In those days we were all happy and full of optimism about the future. What could go wrong?

I was finally allowed to have a regular social life when I joined the

Hehalutz. Our *madrich* (group leader) used to speak to us vividly about establishing collective farms in Palestine, the land of our forefathers. He made the prospect of cultivating our own land seem most noble and exciting. Zionism gave us second-class Polish citizens new pride in our Jewish identity. At the meetings we spoke only Hebrew, sang Hebrew songs, and danced the horah and other joyous Middle Eastern dances. We did not have a real country to go to, but the Jewish settlement in Palestine was the address for all our youthful hopes and dreams.

I was caught up in the Zionist wave and looked forward to emigrating to a place where the people would be as warm as the climate. In Palestine every stone I moved, every tree I planted would link me to a long, glorious past and to a bright new future for my people.

Enemies at the Gates

The Germans had other plans for me and my people. On September 1, 1939, my world went up in the smoke of thousands of cannons, rockets, and bombs. The Polish army collapsed under the blitzkrieg after two short weeks, and German troops and vehicles flooded the area. Then one night they suddenly disappeared. Before we could celebrate our good fortune the Soviet army took their place. The exchange of occupiers, we learned, resulted from negotiations between Hitler and Stalin. The Bug River, only three kilometers away, became the new Russian-German border.

For twenty-five months the people of Siemiatycze adjusted to life under Soviet rule.* Our immediate living conditions did not deteriorate dramatically, but our wealthier neighbors suffered terribly. For the crime of capitalism, industrialists and large-scale employers were de-

---

* On August 23, 1939, Germany entered a nonaggression pact with the Soviet Union. The treaty, signed by foreign ministers Joachim von Ribbentrop (1893–1946) and Viacheslav Molotov (1890–1986), contained a secret protocol dividing Poland into German and Soviet spheres of influence and cleared the way for Germany's invasion of Poland on September 1. Soviet troops entered Poland on September 17, and the Germans retreated to the Bug River. Siemiatycze was in the Soviet zone, absorbing some 2,000 refugees who fled the German occupation.

ported to the depths of Siberia—never to be heard from again. Their assets were confiscated, and their "liberated" workers went hungry.

If Father had had more employees we would have suffered the same fate. Fortunately, our business was small enough to pass for a family enterprise. Now, however, my father and brother had to struggle along by themselves. At school we were forced to study Russian instead of Polish. It was then that the principal of my school discovered my talent for design and recommended me for study in Moscow. I felt honored, eager to make the best of the situation. I had no compunctions about cooperating with our Russian occupiers.

My stepmother could not tolerate my cheerfulness. How dare I be happy about finally being appreciated when the world was in such an unsettled state. I kept a smile on my face and tried to help people whenever I could. I did not understand the precariousness of our situation with the Nazis just a few kilometers away.

Our town was beginning to swell with Jewish refugees from across the river. Thousands of Jews fled the German zone of occupation and came to Siemiatycze, distrusting the Nazis even before their brutal policies became widely known. The town's regular relief organizations were inadequate to deal with the sudden crush of demands. Refugee families made the rounds looking for temporary shelter, and we put up quite a few in our home and fur factory. Father could not turn people away, especially when they clearly did not have the means to buy even the most meager provisions.

Those refugees fortunate enough to have special skills or professions were allowed to remain and establish Soviet citizenship. Most, however, were forced to continue their flight deeper into the Russian zone to lessen their chances of being caught and returned to German jurisdiction. Some refugees stayed in our home for weeks or even months. They needed time to battle the Russian bureaucracy for the Soviet citizenship that could save their lives.

The tidal wave of refugees lasted more than six months. Several hundred people must have passed through our door. My father spent his savings to make sure there were large pots of food cooking at all times and to supply our "guests" with blankets. When we ran out of makeshift bedding he used every sheepskin in the workshop; when these were gone he grabbed finished coats off the racks. He took whatever was available to make sure that everyone staying with us was as comfortable as possible before allowing himself to get some sleep.

Of course, my family's privacy and well-being were severely compromised during this time. Going to the bathroom in the middle of the night meant stepping over dozens of strangers. While we needed more revenue than ever during the war, Father's humanitarian efforts cost him much work time, and our finances were further drained when customers returned even our finest coats, complaining about lice.

Not everyone who benefited from our kindness repaid us with respectful gratitude. One freezing cold night in the winter of 1939 my father awoke to see one of his homeless charges cutting up the sheepskin he had been given to sleep on. The man was using the strips to line his boots to keep his feet warm. The next day he left for Białystok with only a good-bye. Father could have confronted the man and demanded some compensation or, at least, an admission of guilt. Gentleman that he was, Father simply blessed him and wished him a safe journey.

Perhaps Father's empathy for these refugees was so keen because he himself had relatives in the German occupation zone. He would hear occasionally from someone who knew them, and in this way he learned that they had not been able to escape. He finally hired a Polish wagoner and succeeded in smuggling out his relatives, though it cost him a fortune in bribes. Coming to join our family were Father's two sisters and their families. The house became more crowded than ever, but at least now I could get to know my cousins.

My older aunt's name was Perl. She was married to Menachem Weinberg. Their daughters were called Hana and Brucha. Father's younger sister was Hafcha Pszyswa. Her husband, Srulky, had been drafted into the Polish army. No one knew his fate, but at best we thought he must be in some German prisoner-of-war camp. They had two girls, Bracha and Bluma, and a son, Yitzchok. I never really got to know my cousins, however, because we were separated after a traumatic event in the summer of 1940.

One Friday night the Russian police knocked on our door and demanded we turn over to them all the refugees in our home. They seemed to know about our relatives from the German zone and had trucks waiting to take them away. No amount of pleading would help. It was a mass deportation. Since everyone was hosting some related or unrelated refugees, the whole town felt the loss. The refugees were rounded up and taken to the railroad station for relocation to the Soviet Union. No specific destination was given.

It was a traumatic night of crying and screaming. There was nothing we could do for these poor souls who were so rushed that they did not have time to pack clothes or food. Instead of Sabbath eve it felt more like Yom Kippur. The town's rabbi knew it was a life-threatening situation for the deportees so he allowed us to break the Sabbath to help them. He promised us not only G-d's forgiveness but G-d's blessings. This roused us from our depressed passivity, and we set out to do what we could.

Father hitched up the horse and we packed the wagon with necessities like blankets and food. We raced to the train station some seven kilometers away. Police guarded the entire trainyard. We politely asked them to contact our family on board the train, and they obliged by walking along the tracks and calling through the windows the names we had given them.

A window soon opened and it appeared that all our relatives were in that car. The police would not allow them to come out, but they did let us pass our supplies in to them. We were relieved that our mission had not been in vain but heartbroken to see them leave. We did not know it at the time, but even the frozen hell of Siberian forced labor was a better fate than that which awaited most of Europe's Jews. It was only when the Nazis marched in that we began to truly appreciate the Russians.

The Rape of Siemiatycze

We did not have long to wait for our introduction to the Third Reich. On June 23, 1941, our border town came under a German surprise attack.* That Saturday night was one continuous artillery bombardment. The heavy barrage leveled much of the part of town where Russian soldiers and their families lived. The bombs also killed many civilians, young and old, including some of my friends from school. We were only three kilometers from the border, so there was no way for the Russians to have advance warning about the massive invasion. With so many Soviet defenders killed or wounded by the artillery, the town had essentially fallen before the first German troops even arrived.

When the shells began to fall in our neighborhood we were all put into a state of panic. Where could we run? The house would be our grave if a shell hit it, and the roads were likely to be battlefields. We decided that the pit in our backyard potato field would be the safest place. We stayed in that pit from Saturday night until late Sunday, when the shelling subsided. It was the most frightening experience in our lives up to then, as projectiles zoomed overhead and shrapnel exploded

* In June 1941 Germany abrogated its treaty with the Russians and invaded the Soviet Union.

nearby. It would also be our introduction to involuntary fasting, since we went without food and drink for the entire twenty-four hours.

We held each other in horror as we slowly emerged to survey the damage to our town. No nightmare, no scene of an earthquake could have equaled what we saw. The piles of rubble that had once been buildings were littered with the dead and wounded. Survivors were bewailing their loss of loved ones and of worldly possessions that would never be recovered from beneath the mounds of bricks and mortar. The epicenter of the disaster, where the Russian soldiers had lived, looked like the field of a large and gory battle. Houses were still burning.

We learned how the deadly German attack had taken the Russian soldiers completely by surprise. Asleep in their quarters, the men had been forced to run barefoot in their pajamas when the walls came crashing down around them. Those who fled the flaming buildings were raked with machine-gun fire. Only a small percentage of the many hundreds of Russian soldiers survived the brutal attack by running deeper into Soviet-held territory.

As we surveyed the scene near the former army headquarters, we noticed that the corpses there were both more plentiful and in worse condition. Wounded and shell-shocked survivors were still being removed from under piles of debris. Mangled trucks and bodies littered the road and testified to the fate of most of those who fled at the onset of the shelling. Not satisfied merely to take their military objective, the Germans sought to make sure that few trucks or troops would be available to resist them at a later date.

The next day brought further bombardment along the main escape route. The ample Russian military presence in Siemiatycze was reduced to a memory. German troops marched on the roads without a hint of opposition. For the moment they seemed uninterested in us civilians, but we feared their utter disregard for human life. If they could smash Poles like so much chaff, how would they treat Jews? The smiling faces of the first German troops did little to diminish our dark foreboding. They sang "Wenn jüdisch Blut von Messer spritzt, dann Gehts doppelt so Gut" (When Jewish blood spurts from the knife, then all goes twice as well) and their anthem, "Deutchland über Alles" (Germany above all), with equal patriotic fervor.

As we slunk back to our homes we could hardly believe the behavior of many of our Polish neighbors. They hugged and kissed the German soldiers as though they were liberators instead of murderous invaders. Polish girls presented the Nazis with bouquets of flowers and marched arm in arm with them. But the cruel marchers had other plans for Jewish girls. As they passed through the Jewish quarter the Germans dragged girls screaming from their homes. We discovered later that these girls were raped and then murdered. And so we Jews all felt violated and defenseless, with even our own fellow victims, the Poles, on the side of the conquerors.

The Nazi occupation began with acts of blatant looting. Individually and in small groups, German soldiers burst into Jewish homes and took whatever valuables they could carry out easily. While the officers did not sanction these acts, it was clear that the Germans were now the law—or the lack of it—and it was useless, even perilous, to resist. These supermen of the Third Reich tore through Jewish homes like hungry animals. The Nazi foot soldiers realized that ransacking Jewish property would be their last chance for rest and recreation before months of hard service on the Russian front. Propaganda assured them that all Jews hid fortunes of gold in their homes, so all they had to do was to keep threatening, beating, and killing until the cursed Jews gave them the riches that rightfully belonged to them as Aryan victims of Jewish deviousness.

These troops were not like the disciplined soldiers stationed in the ghettos, camps, and occupied towns. They had been rolling through Polish territory for months, killing civilians as well as enemy soldiers. They had met little resistance in their blitzkrieg and were quite drunk with their invincibility. Only when too much success brought them to Russia's population centers, Stalingrad and Moscow, were the Germans stopped by brutal weather and stiff resistance.

But we were an eternity away from hearing about the eventual German setbacks. Wave upon wave of German infantry washed over us, until one morning we noticed a new color of German uniform. On these brown uniforms was the death's head symbol of the Gestapo. Together with a new German *Bürgermeister* (mayor) the Gestapo had arrived to bring order to our occupied town. It soon became clear that the German idea of order primarily concerned the "Jewish problem." With the help of our Polish neighbors, who now turned their intimacy with us into a weapon, the Germans rounded up all young Jewish men between the ages of sixteen and thirty-five, supposedly to send them to a work camp.

We witnessed German officials dragging away Jewish sons, husbands, and fathers amid heartrending cries for lost loved ones. The soldiers struck left and right, callously bloodying the faces of the young men and their protesting families. The victims were right to fight and scream, because no one from this "work detail" would ever be heard from again. The Germans and their Polish helpers also sought to remove the educated leadership of the community. Our beloved family physician, Dr. Gelbaum, was one of six men falsely accused of being Communists and taken way. That was the last we heard of them.

With one thinly veiled ruse the occupiers stripped us of the defense of our young men. The Germans could now increase our misery and effect our orderly disappearance. After some days of respite the Nazis returned for the rest of our able-bodied men, my father among them. They rushed into our homes, pointing their rifles and screaming, "Out with you, filthy Jewish swine!" They carried out the operation at a frenzied pace, as if hurrying to round up animals before a coming storm scattered the herd.

The men were taken to the Siemiatycze railroad station and placed against a long brick wall. Forced to stand with their arms against the wall all day and all night, they were cut with razor blades if they moved even slightly. The Gestapo and their Polish friends took turns torturing the Jews with sharp pieces of steel and the toes of their boots.

I was able to track our men down, and I watched in horror from afar as they were tortured. I recognized my father and prayed for his safety. I went home several times, returning to the railroad station to slip food to my father and the others. An entire week went by before the men were allowed to go home. They were bloodied and broken, but the town's Jewish families were relieved to see them come back alive.

My brother avoided this ordeal by hiding in the fur factory under a pile of sheepskin coats. The Germans had his name on their lists and they searched for him all over. They would have discovered him too if it were not for a miracle. Our dog, a German shepherd named Ruset-ka, was keeping my brother company beside the pile of coats. When the Germans came in, Rusetka growled and jumped at them, knocking one to the ground. The Nazis could have shot the dog and continued their search. Instead, they became frightened and left.

For the moment we thanked G-d that our family was intact. But before we could feel too comfortable the German-appointed mayor of our occupied town summoned Father to his office. The *Bürgermeister* was a vicious Jew-hater who was known to take out his pistol and shoot Jews on the street for no reason. He simply liked to see Jewish blood. We considered not letting Father go, but it was useless to resist.

The *Bürgermeister* was unusually cordial. He told Father that his skills as a furrier were widely acclaimed by his Polish friends. As the best furrier in the region, Father was being commissioned to make coats for the mayor and his family as quickly as possible. The mayor's staff would provide the raw pelts and any other materials that were required. They would see to any request Father might have. All he had to do was ask. Greatly relieved, Father thanked the mayor for his confidence in him.

Of course, these coats became the most important professional task of Father's life. He quickly calculated what materials he lacked because of the war's disruption of normal supply routes and dutifully set off for the *Bürgermeister*'s office to inform the staff. But the German and Polish police who intercepted him would hear nothing of a Jew having official business with the mayor. Half a dozen of them laid Father across a table, beat him senseless with metal shovels, and left him to die. The Gestapo summoned the Jewish police to wrap the furrier in a sheet and prepare him for burial. And so the police brought Father home, carrying him in a sheet like a corpse.

But Father was a fighter, and he did not die. G-d kept him alive to be with us a while longer. His back was badly bruised, and he required many compresses and much bed rest. But he slowly regained his strength.

The Funeral

$\mathcal{M}$eanwhile, the Nazis hit us with a new set of harsh restrictions. A curfew allowed Jews on the streets only from one to three P.M. When Jews did go outside they could walk only in the middle of the street, the sidewalks being reserved for Aryans, and they had to wear a yellow star sewn to the front and back of their garments. A Jew discovered without this star would be executed on the spot.

The posted laws changed with dizzying frequency. To survive we had to hang on the Nazis every word. The restrictions grew increasingly difficult and our prospects grew dimmer. One decree stipulated that our homes must be painted with a large yellow patch. Our tormentors wanted to make certain that we were easy targets for further looting and persecution. After an evening spent getting drunk at the local pub or at the home of their Polish girlfriends, the Nazis would stagger over to a house with a yellow patch and demand entry by knocking loudly on the door or windows. If a response did not come quickly, the Germans would smash the door in and terrorize the sleepy inhabitants more than usual. We could only pray to G-d for the strength to endure the tyranny of the Pharaoh of Berlin and his hordes of evil henchmen.

It did not take long for the yellow sign on our house to attract trouble as a flame does a moth. A group of drunken German soldiers came knocking on our doors and windows late one night. Not waiting for us to respond, they battered their way in with the butts of their rifles and then turned the barrels on us. We cowered together in a corner, still in our nightclothes. The Nazis reeked of alcohol as they threatened us and ransacked the house in search of valuables.

These cretins had obviously heard the rumor that every Jewish home was full of hidden gold, and they were determined to have their share. We had long since been robbed even of silverware, so they found nothing. They shouted at us in their frustration, and I feared they would molest, rape, or kill me. They were the law. There was no protection against German soldiers on or off duty, with or without their greedy Polish friends, who had no racial qualms about raping an *untermensch* (a subhuman Jew). On this night we were lucky to escape without bloodshed or violation of our bodies.

Soon after this incident the Germans staged a townwide spectacle for their own amusement. Posters announced a massive civic beautification project that was to center around the demolition of the large statue of Lenin, the Communist leader. Attendance was mandatory, so we knew this ceremony would be another display of German power and Jewish helplessness. The Germans and Poles came dressed in their finest clothes, as though attending an opera. Knowing their taste in "cultural" entertainment, we feared a mass atrocity.

To the delight of the non-Jewish crowd, the Germans ordered the town's Jewish men to carry out the difficult job of destroying the massive granite statue. Surrounded by Germans and Poles who beat and screamed at them, our men finally succeeded in hacking the statue apart with the axes and lesser tools provided. Throughout the ordeal the crowd took photographs and cheered as if at a royal wedding. With the Jews having no statues of religious figures, the Christians must have considered this staged demolition of a granite Lenin to be as wicked as forcing Catholics to destroy a statue of Jesus or Mary. Of course, most Polish Jews opposed or were indifferent to Communism, and it was only German propaganda that saw them as devotees of Marx and Lenin.

While badly conceived, the spectacle was choreographed by the Germans with the finest precision. Our men were forced to load funeral wagons with the granite fragments and drag the wagons to the Jewish cemetery while dressed in their prayer shawls. Every step along the way the Germans punctuated this Jewish funeral for Lenin with blows, curses, and the flashing of cameras. Enthusiastic crowds of Poles joined in the sadism; to them this was a joyous family outing. Forced to sing in Hebrew as they walked, the Jewish men sang about G-d avenging their enemies.

The laughing Christian crowd, swigging from omnipresent bottles of wine, beer, and spirits, turned ugly when the macabre procession approached the narrow bridge spanning the river. This was a dangerous place and therefore an opportunity to revel in killing Jews. The Gestapo and their friends grabbed some Jews and threw them over the bridge to the water below. At least one of the victims drowned, but the merry procession did not miss a beat.

Once at the cemetery the Jews were ordered to dig a large ditch as a grave for the "Jewish" Communist god. The beatings continued with each new task, and the cries of the bloodied men tore through the hearts of terrified Jewish witnesses like me. As the festive funeral service finally came to a close, we rushed to our wounded and cried out to G-d for an end to our misery. How much longer could we endure the shredding of our bodies and souls?

But the Nazis kept us too busy to contemplate such deep theological questions. To facilitate their control over us they ordered the creation of a *Judenrat* (Jewish Council).* The president of this council, a man named Rosenzweig, would oversee the Jewish police, a labor committee, and various secretaries. It soon became clear that the Germans aimed not to keep order but to loot our small community more thoroughly.

The primary task of the *Judenrat* was to collect and turn over to the Germans all remaining Jewish valuables. As a young girl I did not lose a lifetime of assets, but I did suffer yet another emotional blow. My father came to me and softly explained why he had to take away my small

---

* The role played by these *Judenräte*, which in small towns consisted of twelve members each, remains highly controversial. In the beginning they often attempted to serve the needs of the community and ameliorate conditions even as they were forced to implement German orders, including those concerning the deportation of Jews to the death camps. J. Rosenzweig, the first head of the Siemiatycze *Judenrat*, was elected by the council members themselves and was generally highly regarded by the community. See Eliezer Tash (Tur-Shalom), ed., *Kehilat Semyatitsh* (The Community of Semiatych) (Tel Aviv, 1965), a copy of which is available in the library of the Institute for Jewish Research in New York.

pair of earrings, the only jewelry I had. All the family's silver, furs, rugs, and paintings that had survived the raids of Gentile hooligans now had to be handed over to the Nazis' Jewish deputies. The punishment for holding anything back was a one-way ticket to the concentration camps. I sobbed over my lost earrings, feeling that I had been left without a tangible, physical claim on the world. I no longer had a link to my childhood that I could touch. Memories would have to do.

The ominous posters appeared shortly afterward. All Jews from our town and the surrounding villages were to be concentrated into one penned-off area, a ghetto.* Our house was in this area, so we would be "hosts" to scores of new "house guests." Most Jews had to relocate immediately, taking only what they could carry. Their remaining worldly possessions would be confiscated by our Polish neighbors. We now saw that our previous hardships had been nothing but a preparation for this time. From that moment on I not only felt old but partially dead. I had just a few hours to say good-bye to our home as I had known it. It would never be the same again.

---

* There was no unified policy of ghettoization, so the timing and process by which these fenced- or walled-off areas were created varied greatly. Ultimately they were mere way-stations, serving to concentrate the Jewish population before its transfer to the extermination and labor camps. The Siemiatycze Ghetto was established on August 1, 1942.

Creation of the Ghetto

*L*ike hungry vultures our Polish neighbors waited impatiently for the non-ghetto houses to empty of their owners. The Poles would be moving into larger homes, with extra room for all. With us it was just the opposite: we had been allotted just one square meter of living space per person. The Poles also must have imagined that with any luck they would find that rumored hoard of Jewish gold under a loose floorboard or deep in a hidden basement passageway. They smiled as though they had won the lottery rather than inherited largely empty husks as guilty accomplices to their neighbors' misery. How grateful they must have been to their German benefactors, never thinking that once the Jews went, they themselves would be the lowest creatures on the Nazi food chain.

The Gestapo immediately requisitioned the better Jewish homes, one of which was next door, so that it was our "privilege" to have the angels of death as neighbors. The rest of the forcibly evacuated homes were available for the taking by any German or Pole. The phrase "Jewish property" had no meaning. While my family squeezed into one room in our own home in the ghetto, most Jews had to witness the occupation of their homes by cruel strangers or by neighbors who had become worse than strangers. The Nazi program of making us into non-people was beginning to take effect. One new ruling after another furthered this program of breaking us down, making us feel like chattel in the hands of our Nazi overlords.

The next target was our remaining sense of community. The occupiers ordered the *Judenrat* to close all the Jewish schools, synagogues, theaters, and clubs. Now we were members of nothing. I was only a child, no longer a classmate. We younger people felt the need to get out of our crowded rooms. Roaming the streets, we would try to challenge the narrow parameters of the ghetto. But the barbed wire was everywhere. There was not even one child-sized hole in the entire ghetto fence—and believe me, we looked. The Germans, as usual, had been quite thorough, and the only way out was the single gate—guarded from within by Jewish police, from without by German sentries.

We were allowed to pass through that gate only as part of a designated work detail. Even with one of the precious permits to leave the ghetto, a worker was still searched by guards on the way in and out. Work details were scrupulously watched at all times, so the double-frisking by guards seemed superfluous. The Germans apparently dreaded the smuggling in of an extra potato as much as any pistol or grenade.

Ghetto residents needed to work in order to get the meager food rations issued by the administration. All we received was a small piece of bread, some jam, and a few potatoes—not enough variety or nutrition to ward off disease or enable us to work at our best. The *Judenrat* labor committee decided how to allocate workers, based on the demands of the Nazis. Making us register for work and for sustenance was another way of dominating our lives. Apart from a small amount of black-market goods, not a crumb was raised to our mouths without the consent of the German authorities.

The Nazis would not permit any social activities that would have helped us to regain a sense of humanity after a day of mind-numbing work. Meetings of any kind were illegal and punishable as treason. The few clandestine prayer groups that did exist were restricted to the buildings in which their members lived, and those who attended were risking their lives. Our crowded conditions made an unhealthy complement to our forced malnutrition. Typhus, tuberculosis, and skin diseases spread quickly, and diarrhea greatly increased the number of those slowly succumbing to starvation.

We could not even mark the Jewish New Year with a few solemn moments to grieve over our terrible losses. On the first day of Rosh Hashana the Gestapo burst in, rifles pointed, shouting for all of us to leave with them immediately. Amid screams and curses they herded us to a large empty area where the Maliniak family had had their factory before the war. The Gestapo kept us there under guard all day long, without giving us anything to eat or drink. We suffered under an unusually hot September sun, with no response to our cries for water. More observant of the Jewish calendar than the secular Jews, the Nazis made sure that this Rosh Hashana would be worse than any Yom Kippur.

Lest anyone doubt that the Nazis intended a special affront against Judaism, they singled out those religious men who were brave enough to have kept their beards and sidelocks. Some had their beards roughly cut off with knives, with no attempt made to spare the men's faces. Others had their beards and sidelocks burned or pulled out, the German supermen laughing wildly throughout the ordeal and clicking their cameras to preserve the moment forever. With many men bloodied and battered it was time to attend to the women.

The Gestapo picked out the most attractive girls and women and separated them from the crowd. We never saw them again, though we later found out that they had all been raped and murdered. Anyone who cried out or protested in any way was immediately struck with a rifle butt or a boot. We were made to suffer on our holiday, but we were not allowed to demonstrate our suffering.

By that time it was not hard to repress our tears and cries because we had already been numbed and starved beyond the strength to complain. We were mere mannequins when we were finally ordered to return to the ghetto. The sun had set and our torturers had grown tired from so much good fun.

The Germans marked all the Jewish holidays with some extra measure of sadism and by reducing the minimal food rations that connected us precariously to life. On more than one occasion they failed to provide food to the work details as they assembled at that same open area in the former Maliniak factory complex. On these occasions Mr. Rosenzweig told the workers to go to the furrier for bread.

That furrier was my father, may he rest in peace, who always stored extra bread for these emergencies. He had access to the outside world because he and my brother were assigned to do furrier work for the Germans. He had larger food rations because of this status, and he was able to smuggle some food into his workplace. It was too dangerous for him to smuggle much back to us in the ghetto, so I gained little from this precious access to food.

I was assigned to a work detail along with other young girls and teenagers. We aged quickly, working as though our lives depended on how well we did. Our job was to clean house for the Germans. Every speck of dust had to be wiped away and everything had to be sparkling clean. We knew that the labor committee switched workers whenever a German issued a complaint, so we were under great pressure to do immaculate work. We knew we were fortunate not to have heavier labor or outside work, where fatalities from exposure and disease were high. We had to be cordial and submissive at all times—or risk dismissal. Too many people we knew were assigned to the railroad yards where they carried rusty steel rails and heavy wooden ties. The men hammered in the new railway ties, but the women did most of the carrying. The hard labor and injuries from rusty nails and splinters all took their toll on the railway workers, who could not stop for rain or snow. Survival of the fittest performed its own ongoing *selektion*.*

* In the language of the concentration camps and ghettos, *selektion* referred to the process by which the Germans decided who would continue to perform slave labor and who would be deported or put immediately to death.

The Bunker

$\mathcal{W}$e went through our first formal selection on November 2, 1942. All those deemed unfit for work were shipped to the Treblinka gas chambers not far away.* A second selection followed six days later. It was a Saturday night, November 7. Clearly the Germans were concerned about the number of Jews remaining in the ghetto, not just their quality as workers. Rumors flew concerning large-scale deportations, and we knew our family could not risk another selection. Father discussed the situation with us, and we agreed to build a bun-

---

* The Germans established a concentration camp at Treblinka, near the railroad depot at Malkinia, in December 1941. Later known as Treblinka I, this labor camp housed both Jews and Poles, an estimated 70 percent of whom did not survive. Some 10,000 people passed through Treblinka I, which operated until July 1944. An extermination camp known as Treblinka II began operation in July 1942. An estimated 870,000 people—including most of the Jews from the Siemiatycze Ghetto—were murdered at Treblinka II, which was equipped with gas chambers. The majority of the victims were Polish Jews, but there were also Jews from other countries and some Gypsies. At first the bodies were not cremated but buried in large pits. Only later did the Germans order the bodies to be exhumed and cremated, together with the bodies of new victims. By the spring of 1943, the camp had completed most of its work of extermination. It closed in the fall of 1943 and the land was plowed under and handed over to a Ukrainian family to farm. The staff of Treblinka II consisted of some 20–30 German SS troops, a larger number of Ukrainian guards, and 700–1,000 Jewish prisoners, including *kapos*.

ker in our backyard where we could hide during future roundups by the Nazis.

We would have to build the bunker in the dead of night because we could not risk having one of our neighbors discover our plan. It was even possible that one of the many people crowded into our house would sell this information to the Germans for a piece of bread. We knew that if our underground bunker were to be discovered it would mean certain execution, but we decided that we had no choice.

The bunker would be for eight people. In addition to the five members of our immediate family, there was a young man named Yossel Fish and a young couple who were cousins of my stepmother. The wife's name was Laiche Nieplotnik (this was her maiden name). Her husband, Yankel Weinberger, had come to Siemiatycze from a different town. Yankel had been an industrial engineer, so his expertise was essential in building the shelter.

Covering all traces of the bunker was more complicated than digging it out. The foundation had to look like an extension of the house's foundation. While we dug out an area large enough for eight people, we had to make sure it would not collapse if stomped on from above. Also, the topsoil had to appear identical to the rest of our backyard, so nobody would suspect that there was construction going on below. All the earth we removed had to be carted away secretly. Most important was a meter-deep tunnel that connected the bunker to our outdoor potato pit. We would have to crawl through the tunnel to reach our shelter.

At night we crept into the bunker, removed and stored potatoes from the sides of the pit, and inserted wood panels to reinforce the bunker walls. We covered the entrance to the tunnel with a disguised sliding door, which made for a tight fit even for me. As little food as we had, we began to stock the bunker with emergency supplies. Besides the potatoes that were within reach, we toasted some bread so it would not become moldy and saved whatever jam we could. For water we dug a small well, and we were able to connect one end of our bunker to the town's sewer system.

Our frenzied pace was justified; the ghetto soon teemed with Gestapo who specialized in implementing the "Final Solution." Everyone was to be evacuated—the entire ghetto was to be made *Judenrein* (free of Jews). The streets were twisted knots of horrified people, trying to keep together with their families as the Gestapo drove them en masse to the railroad station. The eight of us knew where to go the moment the end seemed near. We did not know if we would be safe, even temporarily, but we would not go on that mass transport to Treblinka.

Huddled in our bunker, we could hear people shouting, children crying, and occasional shots ringing out. Then, within a very short time, there was only silence. When we emerged to take stock of the situation we were amazed. Where were the throngs of people who had crowded the ghetto? Where were the sounds of mothers and children, of the young and the old? It was like a nightmare to see so many homes sitting empty. All the doors and windows had been left open and the wind rushed through the gaping emptiness.

Our hearts grieved for the hundreds of people who we were likely never to see again. Had they all been taken away to the Treblinka gas chambers, or was there a chance that some would be relocated to work camps? The Gestapo death squads and the thoroughness of the mass deportation made the answer all too clear.

I felt like the last one to leave the cemetery after a burial. Suddenly the crowds are gone and you are left all the more lonely for the company of the dead. The empty ghetto houses stood like tombstones.

It was not safe to be on the street, so we quickly returned to our backyard bunker. The shock of seeing the empty ghetto unleashed a torrent of tears. All the pain since the German invasion began came back to me. Concerned with their own survival, each member of our group was too hurt to offer any consolation. What could they have possibly said?

After the liquidation of the ghetto, German specialists came through looking for fugitives. Even inside the bunker we had to make ourselves as inconspicuous as possible. Our most vulnerable spot was the tunnel, as someone poking deep into the potato pit with a sharp object might notice that the ground there was not solid. We had to envision any possible way that we might be discovered. We decided to fill the length of the tunnel with sand.

Not long after we finished filling the tunnel we realized our mistake. There was now not enough air to support all eight of us. Yankel, the engineer, decided we would have to dig a few small holes leading to the outside. Small as they were, these passages might tip someone off that there was a bunker below. But we had to take this chance because we were rapidly facing suffocation.

The feeling of being dead while alive was not relieved by spending seven long weeks buried in a tomblike underground chamber. We had no way of knowing what was happening on the outside, and the suspense was as bad as the hunger and darkness. With the exception of a few shafts of gray light filtering through the air tunnels for a few hours a day, our cave lay in darkness. Our greatest relief from painful cramps was the unconsciousness of sleep. With that we could have hibernated for months in our underground burrow.

Gestapo headquarters were next door, and we feared that their trained German shepherds would easily pick up our scent when they were let loose to search the neighborhood. Indeed, after liberation we learned that many Jews in hiding had been discovered by just this method. Jews from the Siemiatycze Ghetto who were rooted out after the liquidation did not merely get a cattle car ride to the gas chambers. Instead, they were marched to the Jewish cemetery near our house and shot. The more I learned about Nazi thoroughness, the more I began to see my survival as a miracle. I must have survived for a reason, and that is why I must testify about what happened.

As far as we knew we were the only Jews left alive in Siemiatycze seven weeks after the town had been declared *Judenrein.* If you could call us alive, that is. We were as exhausted by irritation and fear as we were by hunger. My brother volunteered to leave the bunker to scrounge up some food. It was a dangerous thing for him and for us, but certain death awaited us if we did not act. He burrowed back through the tunnel to the house, crawling on his stomach the whole way.

When he returned he told us that the backyard was full of snow except for the patch of ground above our air holes. The heat of our bodies and breath must have melted the snow. The muddy area should have attracted the attention of the Gestapo and their dogs, but for some reason it did not. It was surely a miracle from G-d that we had not been discovered.

As to his mission, my brother reported that there was no food to be found in our house, which had been stripped down to its bare walls. He had snuck around to the side of the house to the small storage cellar where we kept perishable foods cool in the summer. Not only was there no food there but scavengers had found the valuables we had hidden behind some wooden boards at the onset of the war. Our Polish neighbors were so proficient that they even dismantled an outdoor oven that we had built to disguise the location of the cellar. A large barrel from the fur factory that we had filled with items that might be of use to us later was also empty. Not a piece of fur or leather remained.

Only our Polish neighbors could have known about such things. They were quite expert at detecting every possible place where Jews might have hidden anything of value, and they apparently began scouring the houses just as soon as the inhabitants were packed off to the gas chambers. And so my poor brother returned empty-handed.

We did not know where to turn, what to do to get some scraps of food that might keep us alive. And here it was two days before the joyous holiday of Hanukkah. In normal times we would be celebrating with bright candles instead of darkness. There would be eight days of gift giving, singing Hanukkah songs, and eating special potato latkes and donuts. We could not eat memories, and the contrast to our present desperation only increased our depression. We could not stay in our bunker without food and we could not leave without facing execution. We searched desperately for a plan of action, and we prayed to G-d to give us the right advice.

An answer to our prayers seemed to come in a dream that my father had. Father dreamed that his father had come to him and told him that we would survive. From the Other World my grandfather advised us to stay in the bunker until the onset of Hanukkah. We would find more raw potatoes beyond the wall of our bunker and these would keep us alive. On Hanukkah we would be able to leave, and everything would be fine if we listened to his advice.

Father awoke from that dream a changed man. He was suddenly full of hope and surety. His optimism lit up our grave and returned us to the land of the living. On the first day of Hanukkah we were to go out and contact some of his trusted Gentile friends and customers. He was certain that some of them would come through and shelter us. As for the first night of Hanukkah, we would celebrate it with light, blessings, and even some potatoes.

Sure enough, we found several small potatoes by digging behind a different wall facing the potato pit. They were not warm potato pancakes sizzling in oil, but they were the gift of life itself. On the first evening of Hanukkah Father struck a match and made a blessing over the Hanukkah light. As is customary on the first night of a holiday, he followed this benediction by blessing G-d who "has kept us alive and intact so we might reach this occasion." I will never hear that blessing again without remembering that night. A chorus of seven faint voices answered "Amen" and we exchanged the only gifts we had: a last hug and kiss before we faced the outside. Father placed his palms over our heads and solemnly blessed us in the name of the G-d of our ancestors who saw our people through slavery and crusades, through times as dark and as hungry as our own. The moment offered spiritual strength, but at the same time I feared it was a kind of good-bye.

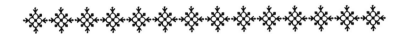

Separation

$\mathcal{M}$y fears were well founded. Father said that we should split up to ensure that some of us would survive, just as our ancestor Jacob had done when facing the threat of Esau's army. Father Jacob did not want children to be killed in front of their parents, and my father, too, did not want to see any of us harmed. He said he was too old to run to the woods to join up with partisans or to make his way to Russian-held territory. That was for us younger people.

He, his wife, and her seven-year-old daughter would travel together. They would go to nearby farms and villages seeking shelter from some of his best Gentile friends. He gave us several names and addresses and made sure we all memorized them. We might meet Father's former customers wearing the very sheepskin coats that he had made for them, and we could remind them of his friendship and generosity toward them. They might hide us during the day before we set out again at night. These would also be the places where he would ask about us after the war, should he live to see that blessed day.

After long and tearful good-byes we set out from the bunker. We could not afford the luxury of walking upright, however, as we could not risk being seen. Father's party of three crawled out first, while we waited to hear whether anything went wrong. When the rest of us crawled out into the backyard it felt like being born into a strange new world. It was so wonderful to have space again that we almost forgot our great danger.

That danger was graphically displayed by the patch of mud the exact dimensions of our bunker below. There was still steam rising from the ground from our body heat. We could see the footprints of those who had come to loot the house of whatever they could remove from the floors and walls. Other footprints in the snow led to the nearby fur factory and came even closer to our underground bunker. How was it possible that nobody had investigated this rectangular area? How could it be that we had not been discovered? G-d must have miraculously made people blind to that spot when they went by.

With pain and determination we staggered like toddlers and eventually found our feet. The outside air felt refreshingly cool, so different from the warm, dank, and oxygen-starved air that we had been forced to breathe. Soon, however, we noticed that it was extremely cold, two months colder than the fall weather we had last experienced. A thin layer of ice covered the snow in the frigid cold. This new enemy, the cold, was destroying the German war effort on the Russian front. We later learned that frostbite maimed thousands of German soldiers and was a major factor in their defeat. The winter of 1942–43 was unusually brutal, but we had no way of knowing then that it would be one of our greatest allies.

The five of us in the second group had some clothes and blankets that we had not needed in the hot bunker. We also had some necessary tools, including shovels and knives. Still, there were certain dangers we could not prepare for. We had expected the cover of darkness, but the icy snow made it all too bright outside. We also had to be concerned about our audible, visible footsteps. And even if we had been walking upright for the seven weeks before, negotiating the slippery ground would have been a challenge. Each step bought an agony of new fear. Keeping my balance emotionally as well as physically taxed my strength.

On top of these dangers we were not sure which direction to take. For me the only significant geographic fact was that we were leaving our town, headed for the unknown. I called silently to G-d, asking why I had to go through all this. Why had I been born a Jew? Why did I have to lose my parents in this way? What, dear G-d, was the purpose of all this suffering? Nobody wanted to help us. Everyone wanted us dead.

I only cried deep inside. I dared not crack in front of the others, nor did I want to be a burden to them. We did not know where we were going, but we had to get somewhere fast. Our survival depended on it. Perhaps later I would have time to mourn.

About five kilometers outside town we spotted a thick grove of pine trees. This would be a good place to dig a burrow in which to hide the next day; the pine branches and undergrowth would cover us. No sooner did we start to dig then we realized it was impossible. The frozen ground was as hard as rock. We had not anticipated that the ground would be so hard in late December, only a couple of days before Christmas. Dawn was approaching, and we had to find an alternative shelter fast.

We wanted desperately to get out of the cold wind, but it was too risky to look for an indoor hideout so close to town. We chose, instead, to be at the mercy of the brutal elements, preferring nature's cruelty to that of the Germans and Poles. We used our tools to cut down pine branches. If we could not dig below ground, we would have to build a natural-looking screen among the trees. First we laid down a bed of branches and pine needles to insulate us from the cold ground. Then we placed enough branches on each side to prevent someone from spotting us—if he or she did not come too close. We knew that any movement would attract attention, so we huddled together without stirring, without making a sound.

By daybreak people were already passing our little grove of trees on all sides. Nobody was about to take a detour into the woods in this cold, but each time we heard the crunch of footsteps or the sound of a vehicle we cringed in fear. We tried to sleep and to ignore the protests of our empty stomachs. Perhaps we all dreamed that under cover of darkness we would find an indoor shelter and the luxury of a stale loaf of bread.

It quickly grew dark again and the five of us set out to find the first person on Father's list of possible rescuers. Once at the address, safely away from a populated area, I wondered if we would be greeted by a scream of fright. Surely we must have looked like five ghosts on leave from hell. Instead of shock or fear our knock on the door elicited anger: "How dare you come here! If you don't leave immediately we will tell the Gestapo."

We got a similar reaction at most of the houses. First the owners would ask from behind the door for a long, detailed account of who we were and why we had come to them. They clearly never expected to hear from a Jew again. Then they would invariably refuse our plea for scraps of food by explaining that helping Jews was a crime punishable by death. They told us we had no right to endanger them and their families. It was not that they did not want to help, they said, but that any neighbor could report them to the Germans and have them shot or shipped to a concentration camp. Even in the churches, they told us, the priests warned solemnly against helping Jews. Our defeat and humiliation was complete.

We considered ending the agony by giving ourselves up to the Gestapo. We were hunted from all sides, our worst enemy being our own stomachs. I cursed the fact that as living beings we had to feed our bellies or suffer such pain and weakness. One farmer did reluctantly throw us some stale bread on the promise that we never go near his home again. All five of us shared in this meager meal—not fit even for the farmer's animals, but it kept us alive. Any hope of finding shelter for our battered bodies was dashed by our one scowling benefactor.

We clawed and scratched for a few potatoes when we were safely out of sight of farmers and their dogs. We found some lime-filled ground near a lake where it was soft enough to dig, so we prepared an underground burrow in which to spend the daylight hours and rest our weary feet. What frightened, scavenging creatures of the night we had become! We placed tree branches around our ditch to hide ourselves. The sound of cracking twigs would also warn us of a stranger's approach. The moist ground beside the lake was dirty and smelly, but at least it allowed us to dig a burrow large enough for us to stretch out in.

The cold had abated, and I went to the lake several times to drink unfrozen water and clean myself as best I could. The beauty of the countryside contrasted sharply and bitterly with the dire situation we faced. Did not the world have much joy to offer? Why must evil men wage savage war against innocent people, branding even young children as criminals to be eliminated?

There by the lake I had my first moments of solitude in a long time. I cried as I asked G-d whom we had harmed, what we had done to deserve such a cruel fate. I prayed that my parents and family would be spared the pain that I was going through and that somehow this hell on earth would come to a speedy end.

I returned from the lake to our grimy burrow, bringing back some water for my brother to drink. We considered what to do. It was a desperate plan for a desperate time, but we decided to risk going back to Siemiatycze. Some of our neighbors, with whom we had been friendly for years, might take pity on us and offer us a piece of bread or even a cellar to hide in. The dangers of discovery and capture would be great back in town, but our stomachs offered us no alternative.

My brother and I started out on our hunger-weakened legs, taking the least-populated paths. When we passed the edge of a village or a farmhouse we knocked at the door to beg for scraps. The farmers again treated us like monsters who had climbed out of the grave to disturb their peace. Sometimes we had to run from guard dogs, so we carried sticks to defend ourselves from attack. Worse than any bite was our fear that the barking dogs would attract the attention of a Nazi soldier quartered in one of the homes.

Our feet were swollen from walking, and winter had given us yet another snowstorm. If we were pursued now, our footprints would be our undoing. We finally reached the house of one of our neighbors, where a friendly girl named Felicia lived. As we approached the house we heard a commotion. We circled around to the backyard to see what was happening. Finally we knocked very lightly on a side door. In a few minutes Felicia's mother appeared.

She was shocked to see us and immediately told us not to make a sound. She whispered that her daughter was entertaining company at that moment. It soon became clear that Felicia's company included a few German soldiers. We were terrified that we had walked into a trap. The neighbor reassured us that she would not betray us and began to cry when she saw the condition we were in. She went into the house and, instead of returning with German soldiers, came back with bread hidden in her apron.

She hugged us and dabbed at her eyes with her apron, trying to stop her tears. She told us that if we were careful not to be seen we could stop by for food whenever we wanted. We should come to this same door, which did not face any neighboring windows, and we should listen first to hear whether the family had company. We should tell no one else, and she would not even tell Felicia. She was too afraid that if others knew we were alive, word would get out that we had stopped at her house.

We swore our secrecy and thanked her for no less than our very lives. We made our way back to the lime pit and shared the crumbs our neighbor had given us with our fellow fugitives. With few places to scavenge for edible refuse, we had to return several times to our good neighbor.

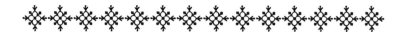

Searching for Father

$\mathcal{E}$ach time we walked through Siemiatycze it was frightening. We wore no Jewish star, covered our faces, and kept our gait purposeful—but still we risked discovery at every corner. Not only were the streets full of Gestapo and Polish police, but many people from our small town would have easily recognized us if they had gotten a good look.

Passing people on the street made me so fearful that my teeth chattered worse than from the cold. Only our empty stomachs drove us to such risks. I recognized most of the townspeople and knew many of their names. I thought it miraculous that they did not recognize me. I even came face to face with the German police commissioner, Rudolph, who was known as a real monster. He was in a rush and did not seem particularly interested in who I might be. The idea of a surviving Jew walking the streets of Siemiatycze must have been too preposterous to consider.

I could not understand G-d's plan in all of this, but I did pray to Him to preserve my life and that of my brother. I even remember praying that He would give us the ability to survive without food. We had very little to eat, but it was enough to give us minimal strength. Besides those few scraps, our only fuel was our desire to survive and reunite with our loved ones. Our trips to town required both the conscious fear of starving to death and the stupid fearlessness that starvation brings.

As we walked through our old neighborhood I wished for the power of invisibility. It would have been too easy for some schoolmate or neighbor to spot us as we rushed with lowered heads through this valley of the shadow of death. We even had to fear betrayal from the one G-d sent to keep us alive. Once when we knocked on her side door Felicia's mother did not just throw us some bread with a hurried word or two. Suddenly she was interested in where we were staying and how many people were with us. We understood her interest in our parents, whom she knew quite well, but why did she have to know these other details? We answered in very general terms. We said only that we lived several kilometers away with three other people. We would not reveal any specific information about our shelter or our companions. All of our lives were at stake. We were bound to our foxhole family by a silent vow of secrecy.

One farmer also helped us by giving us some scraps of food. He advised us to look for our parents. He knew my father to be an honest craftsman who asked a fair price for top-quality work. He told us that all the townspeople and farmers knew Father and that he would have heard if the furrier had been discovered and arrested. He therefore believed that Father was alive and being hidden somewhere.

His calm logic gave us much hope and a new plan of action. The farmer said that we had no choice but to find the same safe haven that Father had found. With all our scurrying about it was only a matter of time before the Nazis or some Poles did us in. He warned us about trusting former neighbors or friends. The Poles were eager to ingratiate themselves with the Nazis, he said, to obtain extra rations or privileges.

My brother agreed, and we decided to search systematically the farms in the area. No matter how badly we were received we would at least be far enough from town so that we could not be easily captured. We had to risk identifying ourselves not only as Jews but as the furrier's children.

My brother and I did not know this yet, but Father and his wife and stepdaughter were being hidden and sustained on the nearby farm of the Lescynsky family. Mrs. Lescynsky was a pious Catholic who regularly attended church in Siemiatycze. She did not tell her priest about the Jews she was hiding, but she lit candles for them and prayed for their survival. She also prayed for her family's survival because hiding Jews was a capital crime. She was so sure that the Gestapo might come one night to arrest her that she slept in her clothes. She knew that Polish collaborators were making a living by turning in Jews. They received a small reward for revealing the location of hidden Jews and a greater one for bringing in fugitives. We were told about Poles who offered to shelter Jews for a price, only to tie them up and trade them to the Germans for a kilo of sugar.

Mrs. Lescynsky would take advantage of her weekly trip to town to visit friends, including the neighbor who had been giving us some bread. One time the neighbor told Mrs. Lescynsky a story about our demise. The neighbor said that the Gestapo had raided a bunker in the ghetto, capturing five Jewish fugitives, whom they then brought to the Jewish cemetery and executed. In mournful tones she identified the furrier's son and daughter as being among the victims. I do not know whether this was a total fabrication or a true incident that she linked mistakenly to us as the only Jewish fugitives she had met.

Crushed at the news, Mrs. Lescynsky worried about how my poor parents would take it. The neighbor began sobbing and confessed to Mrs. Lescynsky that the furrier's children would occasionally sneak into town and come to her home. She never let them go without food, she declared, noting that they had seemed very hopeful, despite everything that had happened to them. Our neighbor, who had not seen us for some time and therefore had good reason to suspect that we had been killed, went on to mourn the fact that the war took so many lives. Even though they were Jews, she said, the furrier's family were nice people and friendly neighbors. What a pity, what a waste!

Mrs. Lescynsky could commiserate only in a general manner. She dared not reveal her secret—that she was hiding the furrier in her own barn—although her heart was bursting to share in the neighbor's bold confession. But it was simply too dangerous to talk about such things. The Polish and German authorities considered the crime of harboring a Jew even more heinous than hiding weapons or having contact with the underground. Perhaps the neighbor would have added that she wasn't sure about the furrier's children being killed, but no conversation was to slip beyond Mrs. Lescynsky's wall of fear. People talk. She could not even trust the priest in the confessional with information that would have meant a horrible death for her and her family. And so Mrs. Lescynsky bore her burden in secret and brought the terrible "news" back to her farm.

Saved by Another Dream

*M*y stepmother and stepsister could not console my poor father when he was told of our deaths. The incident had been described to him as a confirmed fact, not simply an overheard rumor—but in those days rumor was the only news to be had. Father was tortured by the idea that he was in relative safety while he had allowed his children to fend for themselves. His decision to split up the family did not let him sleep. He had thought that the younger, stronger ones would be more likely to survive without him. He had taken a chance by throwing himself on the mercy of his Gentile friends and clients—and it had worked. Now he was hidden in the Lescynskys' barn while his son and daughter had apparently been caught and killed.

Roiske and her daughter had their hands full keeping Father from killing himself out of remorse. They were tucked away high in a hayloft on the Lescynskys' remote farm, so isolated that almost no Germans or Poles passed by. Once a day when the Lescynskys entered the barn to feed the animals they would also take care of the furrier and his family. By means of a bucket on a rope they would sneak food up to the hidden Jews. They could not stay to converse beyond a few whispered words because the human contraband in their barn could have cost them their lives.

48

Father was momentarily safe from extermination and starvation, yet his morbid guilt gnawed at his soul. One day, as his wife and stepdaughter slept, he acted out a fantasy that he had been rehearsing in his mind for many tortured hours. He removed his belt, slung it over a roof beam, and set a noose around his neck. He stepped off a bale of hay and let the pain around his neck replace the pain in his heart. Soon he would be reunited with his children in the eternal realm.

But a powerful dream disturbed my stepmother's sleep. The spirit of my mother, may she rest in peace, came to her and her limbs began to tremble. "Listen to me, Roiske," Mother said. "Shlomo needs you now. He is hanging himself from the rafter and it will be too late in another minute. Tell him that his children are alive, that they will soon be reunited, and that I am watching over you at all times. You shall survive. Tell him I said so."

Roiske awoke with a start and rushed to her husband's limp body hanging from his belt. She struggled in vain to disengage his head from the noose. She then grabbed a knife from their hidden sack of belongings and used it to cut the belt in two. Father slowly regained consciousness and was soon able to take some water. Again and again he asked Roiske to tell him what had happened. Father shook his head for a long time, as if lost in prayer. Then he hugged Roiske and her daughter, laughing and crying at the same time. A light came back into his eyes, one that the family had thought he had lost forever. He knew that a miracle had occurred, and he now had full faith that he and his family would pull through this nightmare.

Father had long believed that the spirit of a dear departed one could act as an advocate for the living. Now he felt that Mother was with him, that G-d listened to the entreaties of the righteous, living and nonliving, and that there must be a pattern, a meaning to all the terrible chaos and destruction swirling around their hayloft like the waters of the great flood.

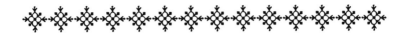

The Hunt

We continued our desperate search for Father, making daring contact with farmers on the town's periphery. Any one of them might have been quartering some Nazis or could have turned us in. Instead, along with a few crumbs they gave us news about the fate of other Jews who had tried to beg or buy their way into a Gentile hiding place.

One farmer told us about a Jewish butcher who before the war had often purchased cows from the farms in the area. As the Siemiatycze Ghetto neared its final liquidation, this butcher ran to his old clients and asked them to hide him. He offered much money to anyone kind enough to help him survive the war. The farmer who accepted the butcher's offer was a good friend of the man who told us the story.

No sooner had the butcher moved into the farmer's toolshed then the farmer grabbed him and tied him up. After taking all the Jew's money, he chained him to the back of a wagon and dragged him several kilometers into town as one would a steer to market. The Gestapo rewarded the farmer with a kilo of sugar, a rare and valuable commodity in wartime.

After we heard this story we thanked the farmer for the crumbs of food he gave us and quickly disappeared. Whether he meant it as a warning or a threat, his account was too vivid to be dismissed.

Many Gentiles turned Jews over to the Gestapo, either to satisfy their sense of religious or patriotic duty or to obtain some much-needed salt or other rationed goods. Many times these Jews had been their friends and neighbors before the war—but the true test of friendship came only with the war. The more we investigated the fates of our townspeople and the other millions caught up in the Holocaust, the more we saw how instrumental the Poles were in annihilating the Jewish population. The Germans could only focus their manpower on the ghettos, work camps, and extermination facilities. If not for the help that the local population gave to the Germans, many thousands of Jews would have successfully avoided capture. For every noble Pole who risked all to rescue a fellow human being, there were ten scoundrels who hunted Jews for a livelihood.

We heard of one such jackal who killed at least eighteen Jews from Siemiatycze. He patrolled the forest beyond the town and offered refuge—for a price—to escaping Jews. He took their money and led them to a shelter he had built near Miłkowice. Once the Jews were inside, he sealed them in so they would suffocate. Later he threw their bodies into an abandoned well, where they were eventually discovered. This was only one of many such characters we heard about and were able to verify after the war. We would come to appreciate the Lescynskys all the more as we learned of such widespread treachery and murder. Our saviors were the righteous exceptions to an unfortunate rule.

The story about the butcher had intimidated us, but we were determined to continue our search for Father. It gave us some hope that people who knew him had no news of his capture. That night we decided to try a farmhouse near the neighboring village of Bochanky, about three kilometers from Siemiatycze and very close to our hidden bunker. Arriving in the village, we made sure that the house we approached was really one of those on Father's list. The slightest mistake could mean death. All it would take was a barking dog or a knock on the door that caught a neighbor's attention and we would have to make a dash for the forest or face execution.

Our quiet knock was finally answered by a man who appeared calm and trustworthy. It was usually a good sign when our appearance did not frighten whoever came to the door. We told him we were the furrier's children and that if he would be so kind as to spare some old bread, we would gladly pay him with our remaining Russian rubles.

The farmer beckoned us into his house. He assured us that he did have extra food to sell us but that he kept it in his stable where the Germans would not find and confiscate it. He promised to fetch some food from his secret store if we would pay him first. We looked at one another and silently agreed. We had already gambled too much not to take one more chance.

It turned out that he not only meant to rob us but to turn us in as well. He insisted on locking the door from the outside, to be safe, while he went to get the food. But instead of going to his stable he went straight to the village center and began loudly ringing the alarm bells, which were meant to alert all the neighbors and summon the Gestapo and German police. As soon as we heard the bells we knew it was a trap. The door through which the farmer left was bolted shut, so we found another door, but that one would not budge either. Finally we smashed through a window to make our escape.

We ran for our lives, long into the night. We could hear the sounds of our pursuers: sirens, yells, and the barking of dogs. At times they seemed very close. The thought of dying did not frighten us, but we knew we would be tortured first. Miraculously, the hunting party dashed off in another direction. Eventually we heard distant shots, and we wondered whether our pursuers were shooting out of frustration or whether they had found some other refugees or partisans. Shaken, we returned to our burrow.

We resolved not only to continue our search for Father but to step up our efforts before our luck ran out. My brother concluded that we should no longer venture out together. The next night he volunteered to search on his own, and he told us not to expect him back for some time because he intended to cover a wide area. The days without him were anxious and the nights sleepless. I prayed to Our Father in Heaven for Moishe's safety and success in his dangerous mission. I felt guilty that I had allowed him to go off by himself. No matter what happened to him, Moishe should not have had to face such dangers alone.

A few nights after he left my despair was overwhelming. I had been having delirious dreams, so at first I did not trust the distant voice that seemed to be calling my name. It sounded like Moishe, but it was full of excitement rather than terror. Footsteps approached and I struggled deeper into the bunker. I heard my name again. It was my brother! I was so happy he was still alive that I could hardly hear him trying to tell me something urgent. Unable to catch his breath, Moishe whispered excitedly to me that our parents and stepsister were alive. He said they were being hidden by a farmer named Lescynsky and that the two of us would be able to go there right away. We collapsed in a hug, with tears of joy and gratitude. But because such information could have been extracted through SS torture, we were unable to share our good news with the others in our shelter.

Reunited

$\mathcal{B}$efore we made the dangerous trip to the Lescynsky farm, my brother told me what had happened on the several days of his mission. He had hidden in the forest by day and approached remote farmhouses by night. Each night one or two farmers gave him something to eat, but no one had a crumb of information about Father. Fighting fatigue and despair, he was about to give up and make his way back to the burrow when he decided to try one more farm. He knocked on the door and a frightened man cautiously answered. When Moishe asked his usual question about the furrier, the man seemed stunned with fear. The farmer asked him how he had come to his farm and what answers he had received from others in response to his question.

Moishe recognized that the man feared being sent to a concentration camp or having his farm burned down, but he pressed on because the farmer seemed to know Father. Mr. Lescynsky then asked about me, and Moishe's answers seemed to satisfy him. A long look at my brother convinced the farmer that the furrier's children were actually alive and that this was no trap set by the Gestapo. Mr. Lescynsky invited Moishe inside and told him the news: our parents were alive and hiding in the barn. Moishe was to stay in the house and the farmer would bring Father to him for a reunion.

Of course, it would have been easier and safer to bring Moishe to the hayloft. But who could complain? One had to be somewhat abnormal to hide Jews, and bringing the family out to see their "dead" son promised to be too entertaining for Mr. Lescynsky to pass up. My parents were not amused to be woken up in the dead of a cold winter night. When told that there was someone in the farmhouse they had to see, they must have expected the worst.

Mr. Lescynsky told them to be patient and to trust him, but that was not easy to do, despite all he had done for them. Why had they survived this long, they wondered, only to be discovered one night for no apparent reason? They were resigned to their fate as they emerged from the hayloft for the first time in many months and followed the farmer back to the house. In the darkness ahead they could see a man in a long civilian coat waiting for them. Was he a Gestapo agent? Was this the last night of their lives? Instead of being bitter, Father resolved to thank Mr. Lescynsky for these extra months of life and to forgive him for buckling under to the pressures of the Gestapo.

As they approached the door of the farmhouse, they saw that the man appeared to be stooped over, like someone who had spent many months in underground bunkers. He had an unkempt beard that hid the shrunken features of his face. But his eyes . . . his eyes were frighteningly large, staring and welling up with tears.

Moishe cried out and rushed into Father's arms. The voice was the voice of Moishe, and Father was mute with astonishment and joy. As the Lescynskys stood by, they too began to cry as the miraculous scene of resurrection unfolded. After a long time of wordless hugging and crying came torrents of questions. The Lescynskys led the reunion party back to the hayloft and told them to get some sleep. This was good advice but impossible to follow.

All night Moishe and Father exchanged descriptions of their travails, mixing joy at our family's survival with sorrow about the bewildering atrocities that had struck our world. The ordeal had taken such a toll on Moishe that Father had to apologize for not recognizing him initially. Father also explained that he had thought that my brother and I had been caught and killed; he said they had heard this from our former neighbor.

Moishe had much information to share in those hours of frenzied whispering in the hayloft above the cows and horses. Then, after eating and catching up on his sleep, he left to fetch me. The Lescynskys had agreed that we could join our parents in the hideout, but it was impossible for Laiche, Yankel, and Yossel to accompany us. This was the only damper on the otherwise joyous news Moishe brought back to our burrow.

The five of us had grown to be close friends. Together we had witnessed many tragedies, experienced moments of great panic and relief, and enjoyed the saving triumphs of raw potatoes and half loaves of stale bread. In our many months together we had shared a lifetime of pain and humiliation. This experience made us as close as family, and parting was difficult. Yossel and the Weinbergers were genuinely happy that Moishe and I had found a safe haven, reunited with our family. We wished them the same, knowing full well how poor the chances were that they too would find their loved ones and obtain a safe, warm, dry roof over their heads. We all embraced and kissed and wished for G-d to continue to give us his miraculous protection. I knew I would never forget their faces or the times we had shared. We had no idea whether we would ever see each other again, but we arranged to meet should we survive the war. Moishe and I promised that we would try to send them food, an address where they might be sheltered, and some ammunition for the rifle they kept beside them.

As darkness fell the next night we completed our painful farewells and set out on the dangerous trip to the Lescynsky farm on the Kajanka estate. We walked through only the most sparsely populated areas, where we were least likely to encounter dogs or German patrols. As much as I tried to prepare myself for the happy shock of seeing Father and Roiske and my stepsister, the moment of our reunion was overwhelming. It was a long time before we could look at each other without collapsing into hugs and tears of shared joy and released pain. The Lescynskys had passed up the opportunity to witness our reunion. It was all the more dangerous now, with the five of us in hiding, and we understood their intensified caution.

Now that we were together we resolved never to separate again. We realized that if the five of us had come as a group to this farm the Lescynskys would have turned us down. Father, the friendly furrier, together with only his wife and stepdaughter seemed like a small enough group to hide. But five people would have been too many, considering the terrible consequences. Only because we had come much later, and because we had been reported dead, did the Lescynskys agree to stage our incredible family reunion and then to hide all five of us. All the pain of separation, all the grieving for our deaths . . . all this must have been part of G-d's plan to keep us alive. We never know the reason for suffering, but the faithful can believe that it is all for our ultimate good.

Despite our fierce commitment to remain together, Moishe and I felt a competing loyalty to the three we had left behind. My brother wanted to make good on his promise to visit them and provide them with some food and ammunition. Even though the Lescynsky family prohibited themselves from coming to the barn for social visits, Moishe managed to strike up a friendship with Juziek Lescynsky, a young man his age. They were able to converse through a crack in the back wall. Moishe told Juziek about the friends we had left behind in a dangerously vulnerable place. As better weather set in, the Germans would likely discover them. Their only chance to survive would be to fight their way out and find some partisans in the woods. However, without ammunition for their rifle this would be impossible.

As difficult as it was for a Polish civilian to acquire bullets, Juziek managed to buy some on the black market with the help of a generous portion of Moishe's dwindling supply of money. With these two most precious items, food and ammunition, Moishe set off for the lake. After a few close calls with police and townspeople he approached the shelter. His heart sank when he could not find a trace of its inhabitants. He called their names in case they had hidden, but there was no answer.

Moishe could not bring himself to run away. Perhaps they had taken everything with them on a search for food and shelter and would soon return. Or perhaps they had been discovered and the police would come back to search for other fugitives. In case this shelter was now unsafe, Moishe dug himself another one nearby and waited. He stayed there all night and all the next day, but no one came. Concerned and disappointed, Moishe became more and more convinced that something terrible had happened to our friends.

We had promised to return to them. Surely they would have left behind a note in Yiddish if they had known they were leaving. Our worst fears were later confirmed. Some Poles had spotted them and had called the German police. When the Germans shot at them they fired back, using up their small supply of ammunition. At least they had put up a fight. In the end they were forced to surrender and were taken to Gestapo headquarters in Siemiatycze.

Their brave resistance won them some fame, and the local Poles had details to share with us after we were liberated. The three of them had been tortured before they were killed, the fate we had feared for ourselves. Apparently they revealed nothing about our nearby haven. Laiche gave birth to a dead child as she was being tortured to death.

Laiche Weinberger had been like a big sister to me. Or perhaps she was even more, because she was there when my parents were not. I was only sixteen when we spent those traumatic months together, and I leaned on her as I was thrown violently from childhood to adulthood. She was my confidante. Her heart was full of goodness, and she was always generous with her calm and reasoned advice. She protected me from young men and from my own despair. I grieved over her loss as I would for a member of my family.

Our New Home

Our days in the hayloft were not long blessed with monotonous calm. Mr. Lescynsky came in one day to tell us that with spring arriving he would soon need the hay we hid in to feed his livestock. He would not have a large supply of hay again until the end of summer. With the hayloft empty, it would be too dangerous for us to stay in the barn. We would have to find a new shelter.

We felt shattered that our haven turned out, indeed, to be a castle made of straw. Knowing that the farmer was running real risks for us, we did not argue or feel bitter. We told him we understood and would soon find an alternative shelter. Mr. Lescynsky kindly offered his nearby woods, small but thick with trees and close enough for him and his family to watch from their upstairs window. We would still be on his land, but we would no longer be his wards. If we were discovered in the woods, no one would assume that the people in the farmhouse were accomplices. Each family would have to disavow any knowledge of the other.

Mr. Lescynsky offered to help us dig out a shelter in the woods, suggesting that we build it in one night to reduce the risk of discovery. We would have to stay well hidden because people occasionally took shortcuts through those woods on their way to neighboring farms. We would build the bunker on the same model as our first one in Siemia-tycze. As the last days of winter approached, and the farmer removed even more protective bales of hay from our loft, we planned our summer home and wondered if the Lescynskys really wanted to see the last of us.

On a moonless night after some earth-softening rains we began excavating our bunker in an area of the woods through which people were least likely to walk. We reinforced the walls with wooden slats so that they would not collapse if someone walked over them, and we paneled each side with wood. We worked quickly. Mr. Lescynsky helped us with crucial things, like moving the excavated earth to a place where it would not raise suspicions. We had to have an opening, which we covered with a piece of wood camouflaged with forest debris. We spread branches and heaps of decaying leaves around to hide any trace of our work and to make any approach to our hideout a noisy one.

Our new bunker was nothing like the hayloft, where we had had room to move about. The five of us were now buried in a "coffin" measuring about two and a half meters by one meter. Most of the time we lay down, packed together like sardines. We could sit up, but there wasn't enough room to crouch, much less stand.

We ate very little, two potatoes a day and sometimes two ounces of bread. For liquid we had a cup of soup. When the Lescynskys used their backyard boiler to make feed for their livestock they would throw an extra ten potatoes in the pot for our family. As small as our stomachs must have been, we were always hungry. Once a mouse tried to take my precious piece of bread. In better times I would have fed the creature, but now I chased it away. After all, the mouse was better off than I was. It was free to wander about and find food elsewhere.

To keep our sanity we would occasionally emerge from our underground shelter, maintaining a sharp lookout for passersby. Even inside we could only talk in whispers. Any overheard sounds from our bunker would mean certain death. When the Lescynskys came by they would occasionally bring news of the atrocities befalling hidden Jews. Fugitives were being flushed out all the time, and German executions of Poles and Jews were reported more reliably than the sketchy news from the Russian front.

We needed lots of spiritual strength to keep a shred of human dignity in our dense world of humiliation and sorrow. We had many thousands of hours to contemplate our fate, our suffering, the hidden rationale behind G-d's plans, and when it all might come to an end. We wondered about the human capacity for hatred that drove the Germans and others to such depravity.

I envied the creatures that crawled beneath the earth and, when we allowed ourselves a guarded excursion to the outside world, the others that were free to run and fly where they wished. The natural world offered so much beauty and serenity. Why did evil men have to turn this heaven into hell? As winter turned to spring, cloudy days retreated before bright warm ones. Surely, we hoped, all this death and darkness shall pass for us as well.

To occupy our time we made our own deck of playing cards using thin slices of a paste we made from uneaten bread that we would dry in the sun. We punched out holes and used natural chalk and dyes to make four suits of card. As one of us stood guard, the others were able to enjoy some much-needed diversion. In the evening it was safe to spend time in the pleasant summer air outside our bunker. We could hear an intruder with even more surety than we could see one during the day.

As the harvest season ended and the hay was gathered and stocked we realized that the Lescynskys had no intention of letting us move back into the hayloft. We could not feel any bitterness toward our hosts and rescuers because we understood that they risked death by allowing us on their land at all, as they did also with their daily visit to bring us food. The trees shed their leaves all around our burrow and the temperatures dropped. The winter winds soon ushered in something we dreaded worse than the cold. Every new snowfall meant that the Lescynskys would not come to give us any food. The tracks leading to our hiding place would have been too obvious. We tried to store what we could, but the hunger was fierce when snow fell for several days in a row. It was too risky even to open our camouflaged door to gather some snow. This meant that despite all the snow around us we were thirsty as well. The thirst got so bad that I took to keeping a piece of iron in my mouth to relieve the terrible dryness.

As in our previous underground bunker, the proximity of our bodies kept us from feeling the outside cold. When lack of snow permitted, my brother would leave the shelter and carefully make his way to a designated tree not far from the farm. There the Lescynskys hid a barrel of food for us. We allowed ourselves only meager rations, but they kept us from starvation. We had our playing cards and the Lescynskys occasionally left books for us in the hidden barrel. We would have loved to have a brief note about the progress of the Allied war effort, but that too would have meant the farmers risking their lives.

The dog-eared cheap novels were not a source of information, but they were a lifesaving diversion. One of us would read aloud from a battered book for the rest of the family. However poor the story, it was like a family outing to the movies. For a few hours, at least, we would forget about our underground incarceration. We were reminded that there was an outside world, a world of normalcy, of love. One day the war would end and we would be able to re-enter that world. Right now we were stuck in a horror story, too terrible for anyone to believe.

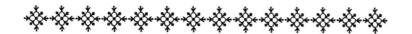

Friends and Enemies in the Woods

$\mathcal{B}$etween snowfalls we ventured out to breath fresh air and to relieve our aching bodies. One day we carefully followed a row of sheltering trees as we walked some distance from our bunker, lost in reverie about what we could do and where we might go after the war. Suddenly the sound of leaves and snow being trampled made us freeze in terror. Several people or large animals were approaching! We could not run back to our bunker without attracting their attention. All we could do was lie low and pray to G-d that we would not be seen.

As they came closer we could see that they were wearing long coats. Surely a pack of wolves would have been easier to contend with than a patrol of soldiers or policemen! But then we saw that the group included a woman and children. These were no Gestapo trackers, but to be discovered by a Polish family would also be a terrible setback. Perhaps we would have to flee these woods and dig a new bunker far from our single source of food.

The approaching party seemed to be looking for us. They must have overheard us. If they were friends of the Lescynskys they would call our names. We remained motionless on the ground as they circled closer and closer. "Hello, are you there?" came a voice that sounded almost as tentative and frightened as we were. "We heard some Yiddish voices. Please don't be alarmed. We are Jewish fugitives too."

Convinced that this was no trap, my brother stood up and confronted our stalkers. As incredible as it seems, they were a Jewish family that had also been hiding in the Lescynskys' woods. Their name was Feldman, and they too had lived in Siemiatycze. They were a family of grain merchants. Although we did not know them, we clung to each other like drowning men to a raft.

We now understood how saintly our hosts were. The Lescynskys had very good reason for being so cautious, since they were hiding eight others besides the five of us. Our small portions of food seemed much more generous now that we knew how many people our hosts were feeding. We also realized how much we could trust them not to reveal our existence: they had not even told us about the Feldmans, nor them about us.

The head of the family was a man named Binyamin. The grain merchant's bearded brother-in-law was also named Binyamin. He had served the kosher butchers in his part of town as the *shochet* (ritual slaughterer). The merchant and his wife had two sons and two daughters with them, along with the butcher and a niece. It seemed miraculous to see so intact a family after all the deportations and deaths by disease, hunger, and physical assault. The *shochet*'s family had not been so lucky. He and his young daughter, Feigele, were all that remained of their family.

We shared our tragic stories and I learned what had happened to Feigele's family. When the Gestapo came to liquidate the Siemiatycze Ghetto, hundreds of Jews had successfully avoided the roundup and deportation to Treblinka. The Germans had failed to pursue some families, such as the Feldmans. But others, including Feigele's family, had been caught in murderous machine-gun fire. Feigele lost several sisters and brothers during that escape, along with her mother, who was Mrs. Feldman's sister.

We did not tell the Lescynskys that their two sets of "guests" had met. (We did not want them to know that we were wandering around and could have been discovered by the wrong people.) The Feldmans agreed to meet us under cover of darkness, and we spent many evenings together, becoming quite friendly. These visits helped the winter months pass more tolerably. As the snows melted and the weather moderated we were able to meet with more frequency and for longer periods of time.

Our second spring in the woods had turned to summer when disaster struck. We were leaving our bunker to meet the Feldmans, and I went first through the hidden exit. Before I could give the all-clear signal for my family to follow I was surprised by two strange men. In my panic I almost dove back into the bunker, but I caught myself in time. I would not betray the rest, no matter what happened to me. When the men asked me where I came from and who I was with I answered in a loud voice to alert the family.

"I am just passing through," I told him. "I am all alone. I am looking for a farmer who will give me room and board in exchange for work. I don't know who you two are, but maybe you can get such a job for me." I was standing directly above our bunker, struggling not to cry out to my family for help. The two ruthless men with rifles, but without uniforms, did not seem the type to help anyone, but at least my family heard me and stayed below.

"Come with us," one of the men ordered gruffly. "I know where you have been hiding." I thought that they were bounty hunters working for the Gestapo to find hidden Jews. If they took me to the Lescynsky farmhouse, it might mean that our hosts had been implicated and would be shot. Instead, they took me deeper into the woods and, to my horror, right to the Feldmans' bunker.

These men were smugglers who carried contraband across the Bug River. Chased by a German patrol, they had come to our woods and discovered the bunker when they followed suspicious noises. They planned to raid it but thought it would be safer if they had a hostage with them. They had been circling the area, waiting for someone to go out or come in, when they spotted me. Now that they had their hostage, they forced their way in. They were pleased to encounter no armed resistance and only two adult males.

The smugglers immediately made the men their main targets. They repeatedly demanded money from Binyamin Feldman, as head of the family. Each time he explained that the family had no cash, gold, or jewels, they beat his brother-in-law, the *shochet.* That their good luck at finding Jews was not going to make them rich enraged them. Like superstitious peasants who believe in fairies, the smugglers would not give up their obsession that we magical forest dwellers were hiding huge fortunes from them. We begged them to look at our starving bodies and tattered clothes. They were welcome to any of our pathetic belongings, but we had nothing of value. The frustrated bandits grew more merciless as the long ordeal continued.

They bloodied all of us but concentrated on the bearded religious man. As the most Jewish-looking, Reb Binyamin became their special target. They beat him mercilessly with the butts of their rifles until his body was broken. We gasped and groaned in terror and pain, but they threatened to shoot us in the mouth if we screamed out loud. The smugglers spent all night trying to force us to produce some nonexistent money or gems. They tore away at our clothes and at every inch of the bunker. We tried to reason with them, even to reach their hearts. But it was clear that these men had little reason and no hearts.

"Please, look at our desperate situation. We are hiding for our lives from the Germans. Look how we are living. Like mice in a hole. Long ago we spent our last money on bread. Now we must beg for leftovers, forage for berries, and look for food left by hogs."

The men would not relent. When dawn finally came they said they would give us one last chance. If we would not tell them where we had buried our fortune, they would throw a grenade into our bunker and kill us all. The threat did not raise a battered eyebrow. We were in shock, grieving the death of the *shochet,* who had not survived the vicious beatings. But without a grenade to carry out their threat, the two men slunk away muttering curses at the dirty Jews.

We felt worse than dirty and accursed. How much more could we possibly bear? I joined the Feldmans in grieving for Reb Binyamin, one of the finest souls I had ever met. He was so pious that he would not partake of the Lescynskys' unkosher soup. Jewish law certainly allowed him to do so under our dire circumstances, but he preferred to subsist on potatoes and holiness. My observant father, who gave up bread during Passover, considered Reb Binyamin to be a special righteous man, a *tsadik,* whose merits helped the rest of us.

We roused my worried family and told them the terrible news. My brother wished he could have come out and attacked the bandits, but we all agreed that it was too dangerous to confront armed men. At least one of them had pointed a rifle at us at all times. Considering that we had been discovered, it was miraculous that we had not all been taken to the Gestapo and executed on the spot. Surely the thugs would have turned us in for some valuable rations if it had not been for the fact that they too were fugitives.

When darkness fell we buried Reb Binyamin near a special landmark in the woods. We hoped that one day, after the war, we would be able to transfer his remains to the cemetery at Siemiatycze and to give him the funeral that such a righteous and learned man deserved.

We all might have died the next day, and without even a forest burial. From our bunker we heard the voices of approaching Germans. Someone said, "Look here, there is some kind of hole in the ground." We saw German uniforms through a small ventilation hole, and it seemed like our enemies were looking straight at us.

We tried to stop our hearts from pounding and prayed hard to the Almighty to save us once more. Father put on his prayer shawl and said the prayers of confession that one recites on Yom Kippur and when facing death. We only had a few moments before being taken out and shot.

"They are not hiding here," said another voice. "Here are the tracks of their boots." We heard an entire German patrol passing over our heads talking about two armed men. They were after the smugglers! For once we wished the Germans good luck in hunting down their quarry.

We had seen the Angel of Death and somehow lived. After all our physical pain and emotional trauma we still felt that only the hand of G-d was preserving us in these times.

There was one other occasion when we were discovered and thought the end had come. One Sunday afternoon we heard footsteps approaching our bunker. Petrified, we realized that someone had discovered our camouflaged entrance board and was moving it aside. A round-faced young man in his twenties peered in at us. Nobody breathed, and the man simply backed up and left without a word. We did not know what to do. Surely this fellow would notify the Gestapo.

The notion of running to a new location and digging a new shelter exhausted us. If our destiny was to be arrested and shot, we thought, then so be it. Still, to remain in the bunker for the next few hours was suicide. We also considered it too risky to try to alert the Feldmans. We might be followed to their bunker and thus become responsible for their capture and execution. In fact, we were never able to contact the Feldmans again and only discovered what had happened to them after the war.

We decided not to make it too easy for the Jew-catchers to get hold of us. We slid out of our bunker and ran to the nearby fields. It being June, the wheat was high enough to hide us. We watched from a distance to see if any German soldiers or Polish police came toward our shelter. We had reason to believe that the army was too preoccupied to care about a few skeletal fugitives in the woods. The sound of distant artillery had been echoing faintly for several nights. If the front had finally come this way, it must be bad news for the Germans. If the Lord only allowed us to hang on a bit longer, perhaps we could throw ourselves on the mercy of the Soviet army. Why would we have survived this long only to be killed now, as liberation was creeping toward us together with the front line?

We lay in the tall wheat, sweating in the hot sun. The person who had discovered us could turn us in at any time. Even if no one came looking for us now, we would never again be safe in our shelter. What we did not know was that the man who had found us was a close friend of the Lescynsky family. While he was no friend of the Jews, he cared too much for the Lescynskys to report them and put them in terrible jeopardy. Who knows what they would have done had they known that some neighbors were aware of their illegal activities? Perhaps they would have told us to leave. Fortunately, this fellow never told anyone about his discovery until after the war.

Our tears and sweat mingled in the tall wheat as we wondered whether we would be cut down along with the rest of the Jews of our region and generation. The sun finally dropped over the horizon and we knew we could safely return to the bunker. If the Gestapo were going to pursue us they would have come immediately, if only to confirm the informant's report and to set a trap for us. We crawled back into our life-giving grave and thanked the Lord for our miraculous survival.

Our time in the open field gave us a better sense of the battle raging just a few kilometers away. The front line was definitely moving westward, which meant the Soviet army was advancing steadily. A few errant artillery shells convinced us to gather together anything remotely edible and remain in our bunker until the two armies passed by. The

Lescynskys had put no new food in our hidden barrel, so they too must have been laying low until the fighting ceased.

In this final period of siege we felt that all our mad optimism might yet bear fruit. The more we thought about our survival, however, the more overwhelmed we were by the weight of events that had crushed us these last few years. All this inhuman torture simply because we were Jews. What kind of a world was this? Where was our place in such a world? At least we knew that there were a noble few, people like the Lescynskys. They gave us hope that not everyone had lost all sparks of godliness.

A day went by without a single shell echoing in the distance. We decided to risk a visit to the Lescynskys and also to look for the liberating Red Army. We wanted to confirm that the war, for us, had finally ended. We moved painfully after such a long spell in the bunker. As we struggled to stand upright, we dared to hope that we might never have to live like vermin again. The bright sunshine of July 21, 1944, would take us a long time to get used to. Perhaps even a lifetime.

Poor Father could not even stand. We were all skeletons, but Moishe found the strength to carry Father on his back. When we came to the Lescynsky farmhouse they were overjoyed that we had survived the war. They had lost contact with us in the final weeks and had every reason to assume the worst. The man who had discovered us had already come to speak to them. As a good neighbor and friend he had sworn never to reveal their secret to anyone. But as soon as the Russians arrived, the neighbor revealed to the Lescynskys that he knew about us, asking if they knew whether we had managed to survive to the end.

Mr. Lescynsky smiled at us and said that we looked like beaten tin but were made of the strongest iron. Though he himself had had a major role in our survival, he was still amazed by it, attributing it to a miracle from Heaven. He warned us, however, that the war was not quite over and that we would be safest with the Russians. They themselves had been told that they might be evacuated. We thanked the kindly Lescynskys and promised to keep in touch with them. We hoped someday to be able to repay their trust and generosity.

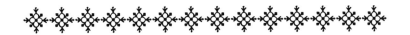

The Dangers of Liberation

*W*e quickly found some Russian soldiers who were combing through the area looking for pockets of German resistance. Overjoyed to see them, we laughed and cried at the same time, struggling clumsily with overpowering emotions that we had repressed for too long. The Soviets were shaken by our appearance. After establishing that we were living human beings, they offered us chocolate and asked us many questions.

We had difficulty speaking loudly after years of cautious whispering. We explained that we were Jews and that almost everyone in our town had been deported and murdered. We had survived by hiding in an underground bunker in this forest for more than a year. They did not question our description of Nazi practices. In fact, they knew much more than we did about the extent of the Nazi program of mass extermination. They were kind not to tell us at that time about the massive death camps farther to the west. One friendly soldier told us that a Jewish officer in the platoon had been informed of our situation and that he would be with us soon.

We broke into tears when we saw him, and he responded with tears of his own. He was overwhelmed with pity for the miserable shape we were in, and we were flooded with joy to see a Jew standing upright, healthy, armed, and holding high rank. Hugging and kissing us, the officer said he would never forget this meeting for as long as he lived. He ordered more food to be brought to us. He did everything he could for us and told us how to get in touch with him if we needed anything in the future.

The Soviet officer advised us, however, to go back to our hiding place for a few more days. With the front line so close there might be sporadic fighting or even a German counterattack to cover their ongoing retreat. Many Russian troops, too, would be passing through these woods, and our advisor suggested that we keep out of their sight as well. In a few days he would arrange for us to be escorted far from the war zone, where humanitarian services would be available to us. He said that we had already gone through too much to run into danger now from all the military activity. We thanked him profusely for both his life-giving supplies and his advice.

As word spread through the platoon about the Jewish mole people, the walking corpses that had been discovered in the woods, a Russian war correspondent came to see us. Hungry for a human interest story of this magnitude, the reporter plied us with questions about our survival and hurt our eyes with his flashbulbs. We thought it was a great nuisance, but even this interrogation turned out to be a blessing from G-d.

Relatives of ours, the Weinbergs and Pszyswas, who had escaped to the Russian zone after the invasion of Poland, read the reporter's sensational story and saw our photograph in the newspaper. They were glad to hear of our miraculous survival and now knew how to contact us. We had lost touch shortly after the September 1939 defeat of the Polish army. We had fed and sheltered them as they fled through Siemiatycze on their way to the other side of the Bug River, where the treacherous Germans had promised to halt their advance. In 1940 they were deported to the Soviet Union along with many other stateless refugees. They had led a difficult life there, but nothing like the living death of those under the Nazis.

We had to remain beside our bunker, but now each breath did not feel like it had been stolen from a hostile world. Our supply of Soviet army rations seemed like a banquet to us, and our stomachs were gradually able to hold more and more food. Almost as intriguing were such everyday items as a sewing kit, something we had not seen for years. I suddenly became conscious of my tattered clothes, but my hands shook too much to hold a needle.

A sudden intensification of the bombardment of our area made us all tremble. Apparently the Germans were not yet finished with us or with the Siemiatycze region. Russian soldiers came to our bunker and woke us up, telling us that we were in great danger and should leave the area. We were grateful that the Soviets, and perhaps our officer friend, remembered us, but it upset us that we were not yet fully liberated.

As the small contingent of soldiers hustled us away, artillery shells began to arch over our heads. We seemed to be trapped. The soldiers urged us forward, telling us that a truck waited for us on the road nearby. We passed troops digging trenches to try to survive the shelling and hold the territory from the counterattacking Germans. Sure enough, the Jewish officer waited for us in a truck on the side of the road. He told us he would not let us be killed now after having survived so much. Riding in a vehicle for the first time in years was a dizzying experience and added to the chaos in our hearts.

The road we traveled on was no highway to safety. The Luftwaffe flew overhead, strafing and bombing Soviet vehicles from diving planes. Suddenly the blasts of noise and flashes of light struck very close, and we screeched to a halt. The officer helped pull us into a roadside ditch just as the truck burst into flames. Buildings along the road were also burning, and the heat became intense. The Soviets suffered many casualties before their continuing advances seemed to silence the Germans.

And so we witnessed the shooting war just as we had survived the hell of being Jewish in Nazi-occupied Poland. Staying with this Russian platoon for several weeks, we moved, rested, and ate when they did. We passed a few towns but often made camp in the fields or woods. Towns such as Pruzhany, Ruzhany, and Baranovichi were all in ruins, usually still smoking when we arrived. Our Jewish officer told us that Siemiatycze was in better shape and that we might be brought there if the opportunity arose.

We traveled about 500 kilometers with our Russian rescuers. All along the way we witnessed great scenes of death and destruction. Civilians suffered as much as the soldiers on the front lines. But the war was now over in our region, and the Jewish officer escorted us to Siemiatycze. As refugee organizations were established we discovered that only

35 of the 6,000 Jews in Siemiatycze had survived the Holocaust. My future husband was among this tiny group who lived miraculously to see the day of liberation. Like so many fellow Jews from Siemiatycze, his family had been liquidated in the gas chambers of Treblinka. Almost no one had survived the notorious Treblinka death camp, and only a handful ever escaped.

The end of the war was by no means an end to the hardships. Even those of us who managed to have our property reinstated had to start our lives from scratch—and we were among the most fortunate. Only three Jewish families from Siemiatycze were largely intact. Most survivors were alone, with only memories of their parents, siblings, and children. It was all the more painful for those solitary survivors to return to the places where they had eaten, slept, laughed, and cried with their lost loved ones.

Even the houses that still stood were usually empty shells, stripped bare by looters. Some of our neighbors were happy to discover that their old furrier had survived. They even hoped that Father would go back to work and produce his wonderful sheepskin coats. But others were not as anxious to renew old acquaintances. Some Poles were upset that we had returned. The peasant from Bochanky who had informed the Gestapo of my brother's and my whereabouts was sure that we would send the Russian authorities after him. Although he had nearly gotten us killed, we were ready to live and let live. Fearing military justice, he and his family disappeared without a trace.

A few friendly farmers came with food in exchange for work on fur coats. They knew we had no food and that the house we were living in was crowded with survivors who looked on us as their surrogate family. We accepted with gratitude their propositions of barter, even though we were bitter about the many Poles who had helped the Germans round up Jews and slaughter them. We knew that we would have suffered many fewer losses if only the Poles had not reported so many fugitives to the Gestapo and had not dragged in so many fugitives themselves. Blood was on their hands. Still, we could not afford to refuse a gift of food that would help restore some of our lost strength.

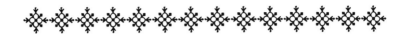

Love and Hate amid the Ruins

One young man who came to live under our roof had been a friend of my brother before the war. His name was Saul Kuperhand, and he had escaped from Treblinka. At first I resented the way he monopolized my brother's attention, but soon we began to monopolize each other's. We were still far removed from the world of normal emotions, but our relationship had begun to grow.

We had not been able to move back into our former home in Siemiatycze because the entire neighborhood, including my father's factory, had been completely dismantled. People had made a great effort to remove all evidence that a ghetto had ever existed. So we moved into a small house that had belonged to my stepmother's cousin. Their whole family, the Nieplotniks, had perished in the gas chambers of Treblinka. It was in this small house on Grodzienska Street that we hosted many survivors and tried to set up a new furrier's factory. The men in our group helped my father, brother, and my future husband with the task of building. With each nail hammered in we tried to rebuild our shattered lives.

But it was impossible to rebuild in a place that had almost killed us with hatred. The more our house became a center for survivors, and the more permanent our habitation looked, the more hateful comments we received from passersby. "What are you Jews still doing here? How did you escape the gas chambers?" Such were the questions we heard frequently from people who must have been among those who had helped loot every last possession from the Jewish homes.

One Saturday night, after a well-deserved day of rest, we felt the full hatred of the townspeople. Carefully planted explosives blew apart the entire house. My family and I were trapped in the ruins, screaming for help. No one came to our rescue for a long time—despite the fact that the explosion was heard as far away as fifteen kilometers. Russian soldiers boarded next door, but even they were too frightened or apathetic to come out and investigate.

We had a rifle, which we had used to defend ourselves against previous assaults, and we were prepared to use it again. But no one came to finish us off. In the end we extricated ourselves from the rubble and removed our wounded. Miraculously, no one was killed, and only two people required hospitalization. They were taken to Białystok, and with G-d's help they survived. The rest of us received injuries of one sort or another. My face, hair, and entire body had been damaged by the chemical explosives and flying debris from the small cement-block house. I was especially concerned about Saul. I was beginning to feel as though I might care for him.

That the seemingly indestructible Jews had once again survived must have infuriated our enemies. We knew that we were fooling ourselves by thinking we had any kind of future in Poland, but for the moment we looked for another empty house to occupy.

Our wounds were more than skin deep. How much hatred can people put up with? We had finally come out of the ground to live among human beings and we found instead that our town was full of more vicious animals than in any jungle.

We understood that the war was not over after all. Many Poles still wanted Poland to be *Judenrein;* they would never tolerate Jews in their country. We kept the doors and windows locked in our new house and watched for trouble. Every so often a band of Poles banged on our door and demanded entry, identifying themselves as police officers. When we refused to let them in they would shoot at us, and we would fire back.

Members of the Armia Krajowa actually killed some of the Jewish survivors in our town.* The police were no protection from these thugs. In fact, they cooperated with each other. If we had not had weapons, we would not have survived these skirmishes.

While some Poles celebrated the Armia Krajowa as partisans who fought against the Nazis, the Jews knew that they were just as bad as the Germans. When they had operated clandestinely in the forests, they had never failed to kill Jewish fugitives or even Jewish partisans who could have been their allies. Just as the Nazis diverted much of their wartime resources to implementing their "Final Solution," these partisans often spent more energy hunting Jews than harassing the German occupiers.

One of the survivors they killed was a miller named Benny Leff who lived and worked two kilometers from Siemiatycze. The poor man had lost his wife and two of his children to the gas chambers. After the war he reclaimed his mill from one of his workers who had taken it over. The employee must have resented the Jew's return and called in the bloodthirsty militia. The Armia Krajowa did not simply kill Mr. Leff, they hacked his body to pieces. It was an act of terrorism to warn all Jews to stay away from holy Polish soil. His one remaining son had come into town that night to spend time with the survivor community. This is how he survived to describe what happened to his father.

We heard from refugees from other cities that murderous pogroms against survivors were widespread throughout Poland. On April 6 the Armia Krajowa attacked us in full force. Their principle target was a house quite close to ours in which twenty-eight survivors lived. The militia fired on the house from all directions and threw grenades through the windows. Expecting trouble, the Jews had assembled some rifles and grenades of their own and put up a gallant struggle to defend themselves. Unable to overrun the Jews, the attackers slunk away at dawn with their dead and wounded. The Jews also suffered casualties, including a dear friend of ours. We spent that sleepless night huddled near our one rifle.

* The Armia Krajowa (AK, or Polish home army) was at the heart of Poland's underground resistance movement against the German occupiers. Made up of more than a quarter million soldiers from various political groups, the AK sometimes aided Jews, though many detachments displayed a violent anti-Semitism.

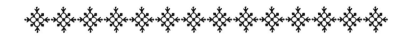

Running from My Past to My Future

The Armia Krajowa succeeded in convincing us to leave, but we had nowhere to go. The Germans no longer controlled our area, but the war was not over. Despite our familiarity with Siemiatycze, the level of hostility was too much to bear. We had to move, so we decided to go east to a larger city where there would be an organized Jewish community. We arranged for a horse and buggy to take us to the railroad station while it was still dark. On that bumpy ride I knew that this would probably be the last time I would ever see the town of my childhood. What happiness I had once known here! What pleasant dreams I used to have for the future!

On the trip to the Siemiatycze train station we had occasion to use one of the few possessions we had packed—our rifle. Some men on horseback came galloping after us and opened fire. My brother was ready for them and immediately fired back. We barely made it to the station alive.

We jumped into the first train car and locked the doors to our compartment. We did not even ask where the train was bound—we just wanted to leave. We had to get away from the Jew-hunters, monsters who continued to persecute innocent survivors of the largest, most highly organized program of genocide in history. No matter what we heard about the atrocities committed against the Jews of Warsaw and Łódź, we knew that there would be organized committees for the care of Jewish refugees in the larger cities in central Poland.

When the train finally pulled into a good-sized city, we discovered that had we arrived in Częstochowa, some 113 kilometers south of Łódź. We went to the center of town and asked for the Jewish Council. Resources were stretched thin and the Council had many other refugees to care for, but it soon provided us with a safe apartment to settle into. It was here in Częstochowa that Saul and I decided to get married. Our courtship was both cautious and desperate. Allowing oneself to feel for another was very dangerous at this time, but the loneliness was just as overwhelming.

We were married by a rabbi who had survived the Częstochowa concentration camp and who later lived with us in Łódź. Saul and I were wed in an emotional ceremony on May 1, 1945. Not only was it May Day and Lag B'Omer but also the day on which the Germans surrendered in Berlin.* The mood was especially festive. The guests and well-wishers were overcome by this great ritual of normal life and renewal after so much death and destruction. It was the first wedding in the city since the fighting had stopped.

Częstochowa is a sacred, historic city for Polish Catholics. Pilgrims came from all over to the Matka Boska shrine at the Jasna Góra monastery, the country's holiest site. They filled the main streets carrying a variety of religious icons and helped make the city a colorful place.

As soon as we were somewhat established and it became safer to travel, my father and I made a spiritual pilgrimage of our own. We would never forget Mother's hand in our survival, so we went to Kałuszyn to pray at her grave in the Jewish cemetery there. I wanted to cry in her presence, to ask for forgiveness and further guidance, and to share the terrible triumph of my survival.

When we arrived in Kałuszyn we were jolted again into the real world

---

* The Kuperhands were married during a very eventful week. On April 30, 1945, Hitler committed suicide in his Berlin bunker. On May 2 the Red Army captured Berlin, and on May 7 the Germans formally surrendered at the headquarters of Allied Supreme Commander General Dwight D. Eisenhower. The war in Europe came to an official end the following day. Lag B'Omer, the thirty-third day in the *omer* counted from the second day of Passover until Shavuot, is a minor Jewish festival. On this day many of the customs of mourning observed during the *omer* are lifted and marriages are celebrated.

of wartime Poland. Not only had live Jews been cast into the fiery crematoria but dead ones had been bulldozed from the holy Polish landscape. The cemetery had been wiped away and turned into a field for
planting grain. The headstones had all been removed, leaving only a
series of scars where the graves had been. We were too stunned to move.
What kind of people were these? How deep was their hatred for a gentle people who worked so hard and contributed so much to building
the Polish economy? How could they use human remains to fertilize
ground on which they grew the grain that they fed to their hogs? How
could they use cherished headstones to make decorative footpaths in
their yards?

And so we left the town of my birth with the most bitter pain in our
hearts. Instead of closing a circle, we had only torn open a wound. We
did not know when the legal and financial circumstances would allow
it, but we were more convinced than ever that we should emigrate from
this accursed land. Father wanted to work hard for a few years to save
money to go to Palestine, the Holy Land and only place where a Jew
might feel at home.

One of my prayers to my mother was answered when, after ten
months of marriage, I gave birth to a son, David. It was the most
fulfilling response to all the death around us. The city's survivor community celebrated the birth as the first child brought into the world
after the ravages of war. But we could not stay in Częstochowa to raise
this child in peace. In nearby Kielce there was another murderous
pogrom against the Jews.* Bands of armed Poles pulled Jews off the
roads and trains and shot them. There was no law, no accountability
in those chaotic months after the fighting but before real peace. Kielce
was too close. We fled to Łódź, a larger city with a bigger Jewish community. We would be safer there.

Our entire family moved north with us, and Father soon established
a fur factory and store in Łódź. It was good to see my father and brother once again producing high-quality sheepskin coats, embroidered
hats, and gloves to provide warmth and style during the cold Polish

---

* Before the war Kielce had a Jewish population of nearly 20,000. Forty-two Jews were
killed in the infamous pogrom, which took place on July 4, 1946, and signaled to many
Jewish survivors that they had no future in Poland. Jews began to leave the country in
great numbers for the displaced persons' camps in the west.

winters. My husband was new to the profession, but he worked hard and learned fast.

All of us desperately wanted to establish a routine of work and normalcy to regain our balance, but my husband's need was the greatest as he had lived through more than any of us. Saul was the sole survivor of a large family that had included his parents, his eight brothers, and his adored little sister, Sarale. His family, of blessed memory, all perished in the gas chambers of Treblinka. Miraculously, my Saul was one of only a handful to escape from there. He survived nearly eleven months of Treblinka's murderous work details before making his daring escape.

While our mission to Mother's grave ended in failure and bitterness, we still had another obligation to the dead. Father did not forget our solemn promise to rebury the remains of the *shochet,* Reb Binyamin, with whom we had hidden in the woods. Father had been active in the burial society before the war, and he took it upon himself to perform this final act of kindness. There was all too much of this sort of work to do after the war in many towns and villages throughout Poland and Eastern Europe.

New Visas and Vistas

$\mathcal{S}$aul, David, and I lived in Łódź with my father and stepmother, not having the emotional strength to separate from them. But we were raising our own family, and my father wanted to follow his own dreams, so eventually we parted. My parents finally fulfilled their dream of moving to the Holy Land, settling in Tel Aviv's religious suburb of B'nai Brak. My stepsister went with them and has raised her own family there. Years later my father and stepmother, of blessed memory, died in the Jewish State and were buried there with great dignity. No Polish hooligans would disturb them in the Zichron Meyer Cemetery where I occasionally go to visit their graves and pray.

My brother left Poland for Paris in 1950, helping to pave our way there a few years later. A skilled furrier, he worked for a family named Garelik and ended up falling in love with the boss's daughter. Yohevet became my sister-in-law and my dear friend as we emigrated to France to work alongside my brother's family. Saul and I came with two boys and a girl, all born in Poland, and the heavy baggage of memories— also made in Poland. The moment I left Polish soil I felt that I had been reborn.

After our painful lives in Poland, living in the heart of Paris for six years was an uplifting experience. The City of Light's monuments, museums, avenues, and parks gave my soul a sense of aesthetic order that it sorely needed. It is easier to forget the screaming of Gestapo officers and the smell of an underground bunker when one is with children sailing toy boats in the lake of the Parc de Luxembourg.

After industrial towns, ghetto plagues, and midnight sprints to elude bloodthirsty mobs, how wonderful it was to enjoy the landscape of Paris and the view of boats sailing down the Seine. My children, David, John, and Sarah, breathed free in a land where people were pleasantly polite and where lovers were unashamed to express their feelings in public. We lived not far from the Hotel de Ville, and we could walk to the ballet and concerts.

How would the Polish farmers who spat on us feel if they knew that we had strolled through the great châteaus and palaces of Versailles? We who had once envied the comforts of hogs now enjoyed the furniture and gardens of kings. Memories of the Louvre and the opera will always be with me, but our hearts were set on a new life in the United States. Again my brother led the way to a new horizon, having many established in-laws across the Atlantic.

We touched American soil on January 11, 1959, arriving in a French ship appropriately named *Liberté*. It was a cold day, but we received a warm welcome from my brother and his American family. My sister-in-law's father, Benjamin Garelik, was an angel, a generous benefactor to many needy people. I called Mr. Garelik, of blessed memory, "Papa," and I immediately fell in love with the whole clan. I desperately needed a tutor to learn English and the strange and wonderful ways of the Americans. Although she was busy with her own children, Michael and Claude, with her husband, Marcel, and with work in a music shop, Bella Garelik became my best friend and mentor. Bella, my brother's sister-in-law, even had time to visit the sick in between finding us an apartment and getting us started in a whole new world. We dearly miss this soft-spoken woman of valor who tragically died young.

It was only in the United States that we found out what happened to the Feldman family and the orphan Feigele. Thank G-d they all survived and emigrated to Israel. We met the youngest Feldman son at a survivors' gathering. He made a special trip to America to meet with survivors from our region of Poland. The Feldmans were just as eager to hear news about my family as we were about them.

We came to this country with three children and no savings. Now that my own children are grown and are raising my grandchildren, they must appreciate what we went through to raise them. The love of my children and grandchildren is my whole world, the only world that can respond to the torment of my past. When you, my children, my readers, feel for a moment that you don't know why life is worth clinging to and fighting for . . . I say to you, "Pick up my story and read it!" Consider the chances of my survival. Then consider how unlikely it was that you would ever be born. I survived for a purpose, my love, and for a purpose you shall live on after me.

Names to Cherish

The oldest child of my brother Moishe (now Michael) is Gladys, who is married to Ben Liebowitz. Their two boys are Alex and Milton.

Michael's second child is Miriam, or "Mimi."

Michael's third child is Joe, who is married to Jill.

I have been blessed with six grandchildren so far. My son David and his wife, Suzy, have two boys, Daniel and Neil, and a new daughter named Devorah-Naomi.

My daughter, Sarah, married Shlomo Cohen. They have two sons, Aviad and Eitan.

My second son, John, is married to Sherry. They have a daughter, Nicole.

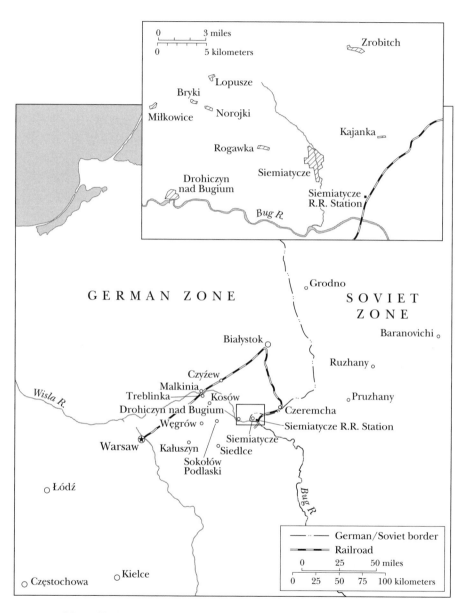

Map of Poland showing German and Soviet zones of occupation.

Miriam and Saul Kuperhand on their wedding day, May 1, 1945, in Częstochowa, Poland.

Saul Kuperhand (*left*) and
Miriam's brother, Moishe
(Michael) Godzicki, in
Poland after World War II.

Saul Kuperhand in Poland
after the war.

Miriam Kuperhand in Poland
after the war.

Miriam Kuperhand with
her firstborn son, David,
in Poland ca. 1946.

Saul Kuperhand with his son David in Poland ca. 1947.

Miriam and Saul Kuperhand with their children
(*left to right*) David, John, and Sarah,
in Poland ca. 1951.

Saul Kuperhand with (*left to right*) John, Sarah, and David, in Paris, 1955.

(*Left to right*) Miriam, John, Saul, David, and Sarah Kuperhand in
the United States, mid-1960s.

Miriam and Saul Kuperhand celebrate their
fiftieth wedding anniversary.

Miriam and Saul Kuperhand surrounded by their children and
grandchildren at their fiftieth wedding anniversary celebration.

Escape from Treblinka

SAUL KUPERHAND

The Polish Academy of Hard Knocks

I, Saul Kuperhand, lived in Poland in the 1920s and 1930s. Now I do not live anywhere. I survive. I do it in a time and place I can only call "After Treblinka."

Before the war a dozen souls made up the Kuperhand family of Siemiatycze, Poland. My parents, my eight brothers, and a sister—all perished in the gas chambers of the Treblinka extermination camp. Only I remain to tell their story, and tell it I must.

I was born on April 30, 1922, to what would become a crowded, lively family. My father barely cobbled together starvation wages from his occasional work of shoemaking in a tiny corner of our house. And you know what they say about the shoemaker's children—they go barefoot! Well, with the sputtering economy we went without more than adequate shoes. Bread was a most precious and sought-after commodity and something I worked for from the age of eight.

To earn some bread for the family I cleaned the barns of a local baker after school. Each time I went to work I brought home a round, two-kilo loaf of brown bread. I also helped out with many chores in the bakery. I do not remember having much time for leisure or play. When I was not studying at school or working I was home sleeping.

I loved school and rigorously applied myself, but I still got thrown out once for a few weeks. It was not a matter of discipline, only tuition. The school had expenses to meet and could make no exceptions for hardship cases. As the desperate weeks passed by I refrained from putting pressure on my struggling father. I eventually turned to my grandfather, who at the very least always had a generous stock of advice to dispense.

Grandfather directed me to the offices of a Mr. Belicky, a prosperous manufacturer. Blindly following instructions, I naïvely sought out this busy man and explained to him that my teacher had barred me from school for lack of tuition. He asked me how a ten-year-old schoolboy was able to find him at work. Then he asked about conditions at home and school. He listened patiently and seemed satisfied with my sincerity. Clearly I was no freeloader, nor was I feigning discomfort at missing school.

Mr. Belicky wrote a note, sealed it in an envelope, and told me to take it to school with me. I never opened it, but I presume he committed himself to meet my school expenses. The businessman's generosity did not end there. He could see I was hungry, and he insisted that I accompany him home. There his wife made a substantial meal for me, sending me home with a full stomach and heart. I had been pulled suddenly out of despair and into a land of hope for the future.

I would never forget the kindness of this stranger who sponsored my education. Several decades later, in far-off America, I was able to thank him in public. I was serving on the presidium of the Siemiatycze Society, set up to memorialize the many victims from our hometown in Poland who perished in the Holocaust. When I saw the elderly Mr. Belicky joining our *landslayt* at the meeting, I interrupted the full agenda to make an important personal announcement.* In front of everyone gathered I paid tribute to the man who had taken upon himself the tuition costs of a poor young man he did not know. My most important years of schooling, my literacy, my entire intellectual life came

---

* Nineteenth-century Eastern European Jewish immigrants to the United States formed thousands of hometown societies known as *landsmanshaftn*. The first societies of natives of Siemiatycze living in New York City were apparently the Semiatisher Sick Benevolent Society (1890) and the Chevrah Brith Achim Anshe Semiatich (1903). After World War II came the Club of Semiaticher Friends of Israel (1951) and the Semiaticher-Drogochiner Friendship Club (1962). In Yiddish, *landslayt* are people from one's hometown or region.

thanks only to this generous man who sympathized with a poor boy's desperate plight and gave of himself to help me.

The gathering stood and applauded while old Mr. Belicky wept with a heart full of memories. Age and years of hardship in Siberia had bent this once powerful and prosperous man. Deported to the harsh Russian hinterland during World War II, he had lost four precious children, his wealth, his health, and his good spirits. Despite the years and traumas we all shared, it still shocked me to see that he was now as penniless as I had been.

I had not been the only recipient of his kindness, yet this former industrialist could never accept charity. Mr. Belicky was given an easy job, though one with great symbolic importance, as the supervisor of a hospital's kosher kitchen. At that fateful meeting the proud old man waved off my public thanks and gestured for me to stop the embarrassing tribute. But I had to thank him out loud and, quietly, the Almighty G-d who had kept this man alive for that special moment.

My tuition problem was miraculously solved for the rest of elementary school, but I soon had to work to help support the family. At age fourteen I began work at Moshe Mallach's ceramic tile company. The large, square ceramic tiles we made looked like bricks. These glazed bricks were used in the construction of the heating ovens that were ubiquitous in cold Polish towns like ours where central heating was unheard of. My brother Yakov-Hirsh, only two years younger than I, wanted to join me at work. I recognized him as a greater scholar and told him to stay in school. As the oldest I insisted that I take on the responsibility of working, limiting my studies to private evening lessons with a tutor named Moshe Michel.

I did not resent this loss of a formal high school education because I realized the severity of our economic situation. Father regretted my decision, but no amount of sympathy could increase his paltry wages as a shoemaker. His mother had died when he was twelve, and Father had not had an opportunity to choose a better career. Early on he was apprenticed to a shoemaker. With less of an education than I had, he was doomed to long hours and hard physical labor at the only trade he knew. Unable to borrow the money he needed for adequate materials, Father had to work harder and with less-refined goods than the more successful shoemakers.

My mother had the intelligence to develop a career of her own, but she too was a victim of tragic circumstances. Her father had died and left her an orphan at a young age, limiting her formal education and her chances for marrying into the middle class. Her common sense and intuition were so renowned that people sought out her advice from all over town and from neighboring villages. It was she who taught me to take the initiative and make my own luck. She gave me the courage to face the wealthy Mr. Belicky, and she gave me the resources to survive the tribulations I would face in the years ahead. It was her guiding spirit that allowed me to help out our family when I was fifteen.

I was passing a building where some ceramic tile makers had set up shop on the sidewalk, preparing raw materials for an oven they were building upstairs. I walked over, introduced myself, and began asking questions about their work. I let my admiration for their skills be known and tried to make myself useful. The man who seemed to be in charge noticed my presence, and I asked him straight out if by any chance he would like to hire an apprentice.

Taken by surprise, but liking what he saw, he put his hands on his hips and said, "You know what? I will take you on as a helper. I'll teach you the trade and you can start working with me immediately." It was a banner day for me and my family.

My boss's children could afford the tuition for high school and college. They did not plan to work with their hands. Perhaps he "adopted" me as a kind of son to fulfill his fantasy of raising a young man in his own profession. My new life working every day at the ceramic trade cut me off from the privileged teenagers of the town who continued their education, but I became a significant second breadwinner at home. My small but steady salary allowed me to be like a father to my siblings, and I took great pleasure in helping to raise them. With Father strapped to his little home shoemaker's bench, toiling long hours, he had little time and energy for his family.

Rumblings

*B*oth my trade and my social ties prepared me to survive the wartime traumas to come. The young working-class boys in town organized self-defense groups. These were made necessary by the anti-Semitism that kept rising as the Polish economy fell in the mid-1930s. Many of the town's Gentile young men acted on the ugly rhetoric that circulated blaming the Jews for all their woes. Knots of young toughs made the streets unsafe for Jews to walk—especially alone and after dark.

We called these thugs "Endekes."* When they could get away with it, the Endekes committed random beatings and stabbings. They rarely broke the law in broad daylight, but they did march and shout slogans against the Jews, advocating a boycott against Jewish-owned businesses. The chorus of shrill voices grew until the Christian majority came to view the Jews as a hated enemy, shunning them as a pariah people.

In May 1938 we young men in the self-defense groups learned that the Endekes of Siemiatycze and surrounding towns were planning a pogrom. We met with the local Jewish Council, which sent a delegation to the police station to explain to the authorities that the troublemakers—whom the police knew quite well—were about to carry out an

---

* Endekes were followers of the Narodowa Demokracja (National Democracy), a right-wing, virulently anti-Semitic Polish nationalist movement.

organized violent attack on the Jewish population. Shortly thereafter an unusually large crowd of Endekes gathered at Jacubowsky's restaurant. Our fellows followed their every move, and we summoned scores of Jewish young men to the restaurant. Careful to alert the police about the impending pogrom, we only planned to use violence ourselves if we absolutely had to.

Inside the Polish boys were eating, drinking, and carousing—all the time planning a mass pogrom when they were finished. By the time the hooligans left their beer-soaked staging ground, the Jews were ready to stifle their Polish slogans of hate. Taken by surprise, many of the Endekes were beaten badly enough to require hospitalization. Only the belated intervention of the police saved most of the bruised hate-mongers from a worse fate.

The police arrested not the ruffians but us Jews. Several of our leaders criticized the police for not appearing at the restaurant as requested: "We warned you ahead of time. You ignored our pleas because you didn't care what happened to the innocent Jews of your town." It became clear that no self-respecting Pole would admit to having been beaten by a Jew, so we were all soon released. We learned not only that Jews would never receive official protection in our town but that Christians deeply resented the idea that Jews would defend themselves against attack.

These dark rumblings should have given us adequate warning, but everyone thought the storm would pass us by. Although we knew about the momentous events in Germany, we could not imagine that these troubles would drop on our own heads. But drop they did, in the form of bombshells one beautiful Friday morning, September 1, 1939.

The German invasion hit Poland like no force previously known. The Luftwaffe demolished thousands of crucial bridges, roads, and fortifications, and the Polish resistance was crushed in short order. As the bombers swept eastward, the German troops marched in their wake. Siemiatycze, the site of an army base, was singled out for heavy bombardment. The base was annihilated and the Polish troops there suffered heavy casualties. The rest of the town was struck with smaller incendiary bombs, some of which fell quite close to my own home.

I was in a nearby courtyard when the firebombs hit our neighborhood. The bombardment ignited Mr. Hamershlak's gas station, and I rushed to help prevent the place from blowing up. Everyone's first instinct was to gather together his family and a few belongings and try to outrun the Nazi invasion. This proved to be futile as well as fatal.

German soldiers were already packing the roads leading in and out of town. Siemiatycze's surrounding villages were now even more dangerous than the town itself because the bombing had moved there to cut off the retreat of the remaining Polish troops. One family of photographers, the Tikotskys, attempted to flee in the middle of the Nazi blitzkrieg. German soldiers soon caught up with them in the wake of a roadside bombing by the Luftwaffe. The Germans immediately shot the father, Yankel, and two sons, Laizer and Avramel. Henia, the bereaved wife and mother, became hysterical. She ran after the Nazi troopers, screaming, kicking them, and throwing stones at them. She begged them to kill her too—and they obliged with a rifle shot to her temple.

The vast majority of us stayed put. We had no idea what the Germans had in store for us. They no longer seemed interested in our ruined town, and, to our utter surprise, they disappeared altogether after two weeks. Suddenly the soldiers in town were Russian instead of German or Polish. Siemiatycze was part of the region turned over to the Soviets by the Molotov-Ribbentrop deal,* and we would remain under Russian rule until June 1941. Those two weeks of German occupation gave us no indication what the Nazi regime would be like for us when they returned later.

The Soviets were intent on imposing a Communist regime rather than on annihilating and subjugating "inferior" ethnic and racial groups. However, the end result remained pain and death, especially for the unfortunate industrialists and manufacturers who were now classified as "capitalists." The owner of the ceramics factory where I worked, Moshe Mallach, was banished with his family to the depths of Siberia—as though being an employer and entrepreneur were a deadly disease.

The idealistic bandits confiscated all the factories and stores in town, turning over the furniture, rugs, paintings, and antiques of the upper class to the new aristocracy of Communist officers and bureaucrats. With the stores empty and food supplies disrupted, hunger and long lines became our Soviet comrades. Only clothing was more difficult to

* See the note on p. 15.

obtain than food, and the arrival of anything edible prompted chaotic stampedes.

My father and two of my brothers joined me at the ceramics factory, yet our combined wages barely kept the family fed. We mostly complained among ourselves, since no one else would listen. We could not know that the grinding poverty of the Soviet occupation was a workers' paradise compared to the German occupation to come. With our options so limited it may have been better that we did not know what awaited us. Better the agony of sudden surprise than the numbing dread of fear.

I knew more than most what was going on because I secretly monitored the Polish-language radio broadcasts originating from England. Prime Minister Churchill constantly warned that Hitler was preparing for a massive war and would soon invade the Soviet-held territories of Poland. For those of us in Siemiatycze, on the border between the German and Soviet zones, the music stopped on June 23, 1941.

I was at a dance party in the town hall. After working hard all week I looked forward to attending the party after the Sabbath concluded. Underfed and overworked, I was still young and alive and eager to twirl a young lady in my arms. I became suspicious when I saw too many Russian soldiers near the building. They seemed far too busy to be on the usual Saturday night prowl for vodka and fisticuffs. Then several troops rushed to the manager of the hall and ordered him to stop the music.

The party was over. We groaned and shuffled home, without being told the reason for the sudden curfew. I was asleep in our house near the center of town when I awoke to distant popping noises. The sound of gunshots and explosions grew closer, and everyone in my now-awakened family agreed that they did not come from Soviet army maneuvers. My father concluded from the volume and intensity of the firing that this was no border skirmish but an all-out war.

Father told us not to panic and instructed us to follow him out of the house immediately. Dressed only in nightclothes, he led us toward the Jewish cemetery. Where it was not safe to run upright, he ordered us to crawl but to keep moving and to stay together. Despite some close calls we all made it to the cemetery, where Father told us to hide in a deep ravine. There we would be safe from shrapnel, and the combatants were least likely to come that way. The glow of the burning town allowed us to see in the dark.

I could make out that the block where my grandparents and Aunt Doba lived was burning to the ground. I appealed to my parents to let me try to rescue them. My grandparents were too old to fend for themselves, and my uncle, who lived nearby, could not help them as he was an invalid, wounded by the Germans when he served in the Polish army in 1939. I begged my father to think about my six-month-old baby cousin, but he still refused to let me go. Reminding me that he too was a veteran, having fought in World War I, he warned me that there is no protection out in the open from shrapnel.

My mother's glance seemed to permit me to defy my father's admonition, so with my heart pounding heavier than the artillery I ran toward my relatives. I made my way to their neighborhood with a prayer to G-d on my lips. The horrible truth of my father's warning was demonstrated by the many dead and wounded people I passed who had been struck by shrapnel and falling masonry.

I kept running, not stopping to catch my breath until I reached my grandparents' house. My incredulous joy at having made it there in one piece was shattered when I saw that their house was in ruins. My aunt Doba had been badly wounded in the head by shrapnel, and her baby boy had been burned to death in the inferno that demolished their building. Somehow, my uncle and grandparents had survived, broken with shock and grief over their sudden tragedy. They attended to my aunt, who writhed in pain, but they appeared to be too paralyzed to go for help.

I pleaded with my uncle, "Let me get a doctor. The bombing is over."

"How will you find one at a time like this?" he asked incredulously.

"I must try," I insisted. "Give me the gold watch you're wearing. It is the only payment we can offer."

"Alright, Saul," he said as he handed me the watch, "go see if you can get a doctor." There were tears in his eyes as the first stirrings of hope broke through his shock.

I knew a doctor who lived on a relatively undamaged block nearby. I ran to his door, knocked for a long time, and finally saw his frightened face at the window. It took some time to convince him that it was safe to negotiate the streets, but he agreed to see my aunt. I gave him the watch and promised to repay his kindness when we had the chance.

After performing first aid he told us that Aunt Doba needed to go to the hospital for treatment of her open wounds. But under the circumstances, he said, the best we could do would be to apply ice to her wounds and give her some cold buttermilk. We thanked him, and I rushed out before realizing how difficult these things would be to obtain at such a time. No stores were open. To get buttermilk I had to go to the farms on the outskirts of town. I had to describe the shambles our town was in and the grievous losses we had suffered. I broke down and cried. Not only did this allow me to release much tension, but it helped me get the precious buttermilk. For ice I went to the company that supplied the town's restaurants and pubs.

When I returned to my aunt she seemed near death. We applied the ice in cold compresses to the gaping wound in her head while Uncle Laizer tried to spoonfeed her some buttermilk. I wanted to help further, but I realized that my parents would be fearing for my life. I explained this to my grandparents and uncle. We hugged and my grandparents took solace in the thought that I would be their link to their children. I had terrible news to bring back to my parents, but at least my grandparents and uncle had come through unscathed. Mother was relieved to see me return but was devastated to learn of her sister-in-law's pitiful condition and the loss of her nephew.

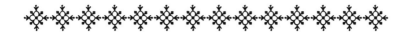

Home in the Ruins

*W*ith our own home and that of my grandparents in ruins, we had to leave Siemiatycze for a nearby village called Zrobitch, where our good friends the Plotnickys sheltered and fed us. These wonderful people knew that there was no way we could repay them. All we had left were the clothes on our backs. As nice as our hosts were, we could not impose on them indefinitely. We decided to move back to Siemiatycze as soon as we could.

After a few days of looking around town I decided to enter what appeared to be an empty house. The Marmur family had lived there, but I saw no one had gone in or out for a long time. To my surprise a dead Russian soldier lay on the floor of the otherwise empty house. There was not a stick of furniture inside—no bedding, not even a stray dish. Nonetheless, this was the shelter that my family of ten and my grandparents needed so badly. I dragged the corpse into the street, cleaned up a bit, and ran to get my homeless family.

I told my parents to stay in the house to maintain our claim on it. In the meantime I took my brothers Yakov-Hirsh and David with me to hunt for usable furniture among the wrecked houses. Father told us not to take anything we did not need or that some other homeless survivors might be using. Piece by piece we pulled out of the rubble of our old home and others enough mattresses, boxes, kitchenware, and mendable furniture to make the new house habitable. We had initially run away with very few of our household items, but my tools and my father's now came in handy. We had found shelter, but we still had no food to put on the table.

My ceramics factory, like every other business in town, had ceased to function, so we concentrated on Father's shoemaking skills. We scrounged around for all the shoes we could find, and Father was able to resurrect several good pairs using as raw material the dozens of unsalvageable ones. These restored shoes became our currency, and we bartered them for food in the neighboring farms and villages. Every broken boot or leather bag we could find became another day's salvation from the widespread hunger.

I also used my own skills to feed the family. A farmer came to our house asking for me because he had heard that I could build ovens. He wanted a large heating oven for his farmhouse as well as a cooking oven connected to a chimney. I assured him that I could build the ovens to his specifications, including a facility to smoke meat. He was happy to pay for my services with food, the only currency available in that uncertain time. We agreed on a price of 200 kilos of potatoes, four chickens, 3 kilos of butter, 30 kilos of flour, and a supply of kasha.

Now I had a job, but the Gestapo made it difficult for me to get to it. The Jews of Siemiatycze were forbidden to leave town, even to work or procure food from the surrounding farms. The Germans were ordered to shoot on sight any Jew caught outside the town perimeter. My family worried about my working outside town, but I had no alternative. I was the oldest child; the responsibility lay on my shoulders. After a week of work the farmer and I made the stressful trip back to town. The farmer, too, risked his life by associating with me. The payoff for putting my life on the line was the wagonful of supplies we brought to my family, the first half of my promised "payment."

Thank G-d we arrived safely, happily delivering the lifesaving food. My father took me aside to discuss my work. He wanted to know if I was able to improvise and compensate for unavailable materials. He asked me how I was doing and if everyone was satisfied with my work. The farmer overheard us. "Your son has two golden hands," he beamed. "I've never seen a better job done."

I was glad that I had always paid close attention to every step of the kiln-building process. I had proven to myself at a crucial time that I had mastered a complex set of procedures. In three weeks the work was completed to everyone's satisfaction and I came home with the rest of our provisions. The first week home I was happy to rest, but my second week of inactivity concerned me. The *Judenrat* (Jewish Council) also knew about my skills, and the president, a man named Rosenzweig,* sent me a letter telling me to report to the labor committee immediately.

Mr. Rosenzweig told me that the German army needed skilled bricklayers and carpenters to construct barracks. He told me to report for work the next day but did not offer extra food rations as compensation. I explained to him that I was the sole provider for my large family and that I would not be able to feed them on what the German army was offering. I had to work for more than a dozen people, I told him, not only for myself. I was happy to work hard for anyone, even the Germans, if I would be paid for my work.

The president of the *Judenrat* was not moved. If I did not report for work the next morning, he assured me, I would be dragged there by the police. We glared at each other and I stormed out.

Back home I talked things over with my mother. She advised me to show up the next morning, as they demanded. But I should not bring my tools, nor should I appear to be the kind of skilled worker they would want to keep.

Sure enough, the first question they asked me the next morning was, "Where are your tools?" "I'm not qualified to be a bricklayer," I told them. "I'm only a young apprentice who helped with unskilled labor at a ceramics factory. I carried materials and mixed cement once in a while."

The German officer at the work site was disappointed that someone of such low caliber had been sent for this job. Nonetheless, he did not send me home. I had to help the bricklayers clean up the work site for a few days as they built the barracks. Knowing that my family had lost everything in the bombing, some of the workmen wished me luck in finding private work to support my family. Between fighting off the *Judenrat* and looking for a paying job, I saw little of home for several days. I did not know that the Germans had different plans for my employment and my family.

* See the note on p. 26.

One day I was caught in a forced labor roundup, suddenly surrounded by dozens of German soldiers. Together with scores of young Jewish men I was spirited away to the battle zone. The Germans took us to a place on the front line where battles had raged only a day or two before. They assigned several of us to go into the trenches and bunkers and carry out the many bodies of dead Russian soldiers. It was not a pleasant introduction to death, nor to the realities of battle. Although I had run through a maze of dead and wounded right after our town's bombardment, I had not had to handle any corpses as old and badly mangled as these. We tied handkerchiefs over our noses and mouths and tried to pretend we were hauling away broken masonry instead of former human beings.

I had no great fondness for Russian soldiers, but I would have much preferred dumping Nazis into a mass grave. These animals should have had the decency to bury their enemies right away. Instead, they waited until it was a very dirty job to assign to the Jews. I could not help but contrast the Russians' anonymous mass burial to my aunt Doba's recent funeral. Despite the chaotic conditions we gave her a proper and dignified burial after she succumbed to her wounds.

When our dirty work in the trenches was over, the dangerous work began. We had to collect, sort, and clean Soviet ordnance, including shells and ammunition that could have exploded in our faces. As if that was not dangerous enough, the Germans forced us to walk through the Russian mine fields after a brief lesson on how to find and remove mines. This was frightening work. It infuriated us that we had to risk our lives to do a job that should have been done by trained soldiers with metal detectors. We realized that we were providing inexpensive entertainment more than vital services. How amused they would have been to see a Jew blown up while performing this macabre fieldwork.

After two days of burying and unburying death and destruction for the Germans I was fed up. I realized that if I tried to escape my chances of survival would be higher than if I continued to work. I slipped away and found my way home. My parents were relieved to see me even though escape from a work detail could mean a death sentence. A bricklayer I knew agreed that I had made the right decision, since if I had stayed they might have shot me on a whim even if I survived the mines.

I had intended to continue my quest for work, but I never got the chance. The Nazis imposed a crushing curfew on all Jews. We were allowed out of our homes for only two hours a day. Sidewalks were off-limits to Jews, who now had to walk in the middle of the street. We were forbidden to shop in Christian stores. One crippling restriction followed another until the Jewish population of Siemiatycze and the surrounding area was enclosed in a ghetto. In August 1942, high fences with barbed wire went up all around us. Jewish guards were posted on the inside, while armed Germans and Poles patrolled the outside perimeter.

Jews from other neighborhoods were herded into our ghetto, and the overcrowding compounded our worsening problems with food and hygiene. Every room housed a family instead of an individual. Every barn or storehouse was turned into living space, and many people began to dig bunkers beneath their basements. My only opportunities to leave the ghetto came when the labor committee of the Jewish Council called me to join a work detail. Luckily, there was no record of my previous desertion. The work was hard but far more tolerable than it had been during my previous experience. Several days a week we worked on extending the existing rail lines.

We traveled in set groups, heavily guarded at all times. Our overseers humiliated us and treated us like slaves. Any wrong move meant certain death. They were the law and they made us into mindless puppets, overworked and underfed. Food in the ghetto was strictly rationed and controlled by the *Judenrat's* community kitchen. The small rations of bread came from a Jewish bakery beyond the ghetto walls.

In addition to physical starvation, the Nazis starved us spiritually as well. All our synagogues lay outside the ghetto. Because any type of gathering was forbidden, prayer became a clandestine activity carried out in private living rooms. Lookouts made sure that worshipers were not mowed down by the SS. Although community prayer persisted, the Nazis saw to it that Jewish holidays were miserable. On Rosh Hashana, the Jewish New Year, we were forced to listen to the harsh bellowing of German soldiers instead of the solemn notes of the ram's horn. Punctuating their shouts with blows and kicks, they herded us toward a large open courtyard where the Maliniak brothers had operated their factory.

The Nazis kept us there without food and drink all that hot, humid day. They turned feast days into fast days, purposely torturing us spiritually as well as physically. They took too much sadistic joy in beating and killing people for us to believe that they were a master race and we were ethnic dirt. No, each targeted Jewish custom convinced us that they saw us as a dangerous rival to their ludicrous claims of superiority. How were these men with faces twisted by hate any better than the illiterate Cossacks who looted, raped, and killed in a less-organized fashion? Their polished boots and love of protocol represented only a thin veneer of culture.

After that devastating High Holiday period dark rumors swept through the ghetto like fallen leaves, rumors that Jews were being transported to gas chambers, that Jews who could not work would not even rate the ghetto's slow murder from starvation and disease. The ghettos of neighboring towns were being liquidated one by one. What was happening to all the Jews? They were being taken in cattle cars to a facility called Treblinka. We envisioned a forced labor camp, another era of slavery akin to what the Jews had experienced in ancient Egypt.

Soon a special battalion of brown-uniformed stormtroopers surrounded us. Calamity was in the air. Mrs. Kapelushnik was so sure we would be expelled from our homes that she decided to burn all her belongings. No Germans or Poles were going to benefit from looting her family's hard-earned possessions. We saw heavy smoke pouring out of her chimney as she committed everything she owned—from broken-up furniture to clothing—to her stove. Alerted by concerned Poles, the Gestapo burst into her home, dragged her to the ghetto wall, and shot her in front of her family.

At the time some thought her actions were rash, but now I consider her to be a hero. She truly merited the proper burial she received as a righteous person. Her family said the Kaddish at her grave and the community honored her. True, she died a violent death, but perhaps her act of defiance, her protest against injustice, kept her from the anonymous death awaiting millions of death camp victims.

Tension mounted in the ghetto when even the work details ceased. The angels of death had something in mind for us, and without weapons or food all we could do was wait, hope, and pray. I looked around with instant nostalgia. Would I ever see my hometown again? Life there had been a struggle, but it was the only world I knew.

Our Nazi tormentors knew that we would soon be gone, but they could not even bear to let the Jewish dead rest in peace. Perhaps our ability to dignify and hallow life by grieving for Mrs. Kapelushnik had infuriated them. They ordered a group of young men, myself among them, to turn over all the gravestones and demolish all the graves in the Jewish cemetery.

Crushed by this sadistic decree aimed at our most sacred sensibilities, we hurriedly asked our rabbis what to do. Should we face death rather than dishonor our ancestors? No, our rabbis told us with a heavy sigh. Even the memory of the dead is not as sacred as life. We must do everything possible to prolong our lives. Suicide is murder. Perhaps we will yet survive to do G-d's will, asking forgiveness from the dead, just as we hope to be forgiven by the Lord who has justly hidden His face from us in these terrible days of woe.

We wept as we carried out the barbaric commands of the Nazis. At each grave we begged forgiveness for disrupting the eternal rest of our revered grandfathers and grandmothers. Perhaps G-d was punishing us for not living up to their standards of spirituality. We could not understand the limitless hatred that our enemies extended even to dead Jews.

Railroad Tracks to Hell

*I*t was late at night on Sunday November 1, 1942, that the liquidation of the Siemiatycze Ghetto commenced. We had a clue that this day might be our last in our native town—and, perhaps, of our lives. At six the next morning the distinguished head of the *Judenrat,* Mr. Rosenzweig, was seen running around like a frightened rabbit. Questioned by townspeople, all he could say was, "We are finished, my friends. Save yourselves if you can." The rumors of deportation to the Treblinka death camp were confirmed by information bought from two German officers. The news flew everywhere. The Jews of Siemiatycze were in a panic. Where could we hide? What should we do? From where would our salvation come?

Later that morning four Jewish barbers were seized and shot. Yankel Orlansky was shot at the ghetto gate as he reported to his job at the mayor's office. Fearing a murderous pogrom, hundreds of Jews tried to get through, under, or over the ghetto walls and run for the forest. But Nazi soldiers were stationed everywhere, and they ruthlessly felled hundreds of the escapees. Only a very few made their way to the Aryan side or to the woods when a sudden surge of people broke through the walls all at once and the Germans simply did not have enough guns to drop every one of them.

I decided to stay with my family. We awaited instructions from our new *Judenrat* leader, Meyer Shereshevsky, who had replaced Mr. Rosenzweig after his murder by stormtroopers for revealing the deadly destination of the transports. Whatever was going to happen would unfold with German precision. Eventually, we were ordered to congregate at a central location, where we were lined up in rows of eight. Every eighth person was taken to a separate line. Then children, the elderly, and the sick were thrown into wagons. Those unable to walk on their own were shot on the spot. About 2,400 Jews were selected and marched to the train depot. Stragglers, protesters, and unlucky escapees received lead tickets to the Other World.

I kept my family in the back rows to delay our separation as long as possible. Those in the large group headed for the train were told that they were going to work in occupied Russia. The few people who believed that story discovered the truth when the train arrived at the large Czeremcha station, clearly headed for Treblinka. Some did escape. Several passengers on that ill-fated train survived the war by paying Poles to hide them. The remainder of that first transport from Siemiatycze went straight to the Treblinka extermination camp, where they were cremated the very next day.*

Those of us who had not been selected were allowed to return to our depleted ghetto. My friend Hershel Hurshes, may he rest in peace, advised me to tear up our house to make sure that the Nazis and their henchmen got nothing of value. At first I refused to do this, fearing that the Nazis would only kill more Jews in their frustration. But as preparations for the final liquidation of the ghetto proceeded, I realized that we had nothing to lose by angering these savages. I helped destroy anything of value. It was a small act of resistance, but it let me vent some of my emotions.

On November 5 another mass assembly took place—but it was a false alarm, the Germans toying with their helpless victims. The reprieve gave some Jews the opportunity to prepare underground bunkers where they could hide when the ghetto was liquidated. Two days later, on November 7, 1942, the remaining 2,500 Jews of the Siemiatycze Ghetto were assembled at the gate. The president of the *Judenrat* was a

* See the note on p. 32.

cousin of my mother, and when I saw him I asked if we were better off staying at the front of the line or moving to the back. Meyer Shereshevsky could not openly tell me what to do, but he did say, "What is your hurry? You are not going to a wedding."

The Nazis announced repeatedly that we were headed for a work camp, but I understood the ominous tone of the warning and herded my family from the front to the back of the long line. My little sister was crying from exhaustion, hunger, and thirst, but all we could offer her were words of consolation. Finally it was our turn to be driven by wagon to the train station. Many of us started to weep, knowing this could well be the last time we saw our hometown. Many of us also knew that this might be the last day of our lives. Israel Krawiec and Hershel Laidak were driven to the station by automobile; they had closed the gates of the empty ghetto. My hometown was officially declared *Judenrein* (free of Jews).

The fright of the deportees was terrible to see. The cries of parents and children would have melted any human heart but, sadly, our oppressors displayed no such humanity. The pleading in a young child's eye could not stay the blows, kicks, and occasional bullets with which we were herded onto the transport. The ghetto police and members of the *Judenrat* occupied the few passenger cars, while the rest of us were piled into boxcars like cattle on the way to slaughter. We were all headed for the same destiny. The delay only increased our anxiety that extermination, not hard labor, awaited us.

A number of people decided to escape as soon as they ascertained that the train was headed to Treblinka rather than the Russian territories. I know of one group of eleven Jews who jumped from the train as it traveled at high speed. Of this group, Max Gruskin and Mattis Tronowski did not survive; Hershel Resnick, Rivka Gruskin, Kalman Goldwasser, Lazer Resnick, and Sonya Tronowski survived not only the jump from the train but the war. Those who jumped to avoid Treblinka and are still alive at this writing include Abraham Wallach, Irving Morer, and Israel Krawiec.

Nothing was more tragic, or more glorious, than the sight of the town's teacher, Mr. Yehuda Kohut, staying with hundreds of his students on that death train. He led them in singing "Hatikvah" (The hope), the song that would become Israel's national anthem.* Mr. Kohut had all those children singing about the future and not thinking of the horrifying present. He is a forgotten hero of the Holocaust, but allow me to commemorate his bravery. May the Lord wreak vengeance for the wanton murder of innocents.

Pushed into a passenger car at the station, my family sat near fourteen-year-old Gershon Katz, his parents, and his five-year-old sister. Gershon whispered to me that he knew the rail line and the area very well. If, at the city of Czeremcha, the train turned right, we might be headed for a work camp. If, however, the train veered left, we were going toward Malkinia, the direction of Treblinka. During that long night's ride I waited for Gershon to recognize the switching area. When we finally got there the train turned to the left.

Gershon began to cry to his mother. "Dear Mother, I love you so much. I never told you this before. Let me thank you for everything you did for me all these years." His sincerity and certainty shattered all our illusions about survival. Many of us broke down and lamented the certain death that we now knew awaited us.

One beautiful young girl from our town, Leah Horowitz, became hysterical, throwing herself on the floor, kicking the air, and tearing out her long black hair. To maintain our sanity we prayed for a better fate, but she shouted the words we did not want to hear: "We are going to Treblinka. We are all going to be killed."

Some passengers sought refuge in something safer than insanity. A husband and wife of the Daitch family, whom I knew from the ceramics business, took poison and died in each others' arms. Inspired by rumors that other deportees had escaped by leaping from the train, I was seized by the desire to break out of this speeding death trap. I told my father of my intention, and he looked at me with understanding.

"I can't tell you what to do. You might be jumping to your death, but you might, with G-d's help, be saving your life. Let me advise you as a former soldier that there are German guards on the roof of every car. They have machine guns and they will only see you better if you

---

* Naphtali Herz Imber (1856–1909) wrote the words to "Hatikvah." First published in 1886, the song had become the unofficial anthem of the Zionist movement by around 1905. The Zionist Congress of 1933 made its status official.

run. If you decide to jump, stay still and close to the ground until the train is out of sight. Let me know before you jump, but I don't want to be facing you . . . in case you don't make it."

I thanked my father for his understanding and his calm advice. I went over to my mother and explained why I had to take this last chance to save myself. My little sister, Sarale, was nearby and overheard everything. She hugged and kissed me, crying and imploring me not to leave them.

"Father and Mother are old and sick. They are very tired and weak now. You are the oldest brother. You are like our parent. How will you take care of us if you jump out to save yourself? How would you do it? Please answer me."

I was thunderstruck by this seven-year-old's logic, and I could not find an adequate answer to her question. If I survived and they did not, I would never be able to live with myself for lack of an answer. My mother urged me to do what I felt was right, and I finally decided what that was. I looked my little sister in her eyes and told her, "Wherever you go, I will go. I'm staying on this train with the whole family."

Daylight began to come through the tiny windows, and already we could see groups of laborers wearing the Star of David. We were near Treblinka's gas chambers, but at least the sight of the workers confirmed that we would work for the devil for some time before being cast into hell. The train slowed and then stood still for a couple of hours. Then we started to move again, passing through a thick pine forest. In another time we might have been tourists enjoying the lovely scenery.

Suddenly the train stopped and Ukrainian guards pulled open the heavy doors and began shouting. There were also Gestapo men with snarling German shepherds and flailing batons. "Everybody off," they shouted in German. "Men to the right side. Women and children to the left." Our family was separated.

I can still picture Siemiatycze's spiritual leader, Rabbi Gerstein, being helped off the train by his loyal friend Kalman Ribowsky. The rabbi was squinting up at the sky and repeating the *shema yisrael* prayer: "Hear O' Israel, the Lord our G-d, the Lord is one."

My family was no longer together. Except for two of my brothers, I never saw any of them again after we were separated while leaving the train. I was among 150 selected for work in Treblinka I, but nine members of my family were marched off to Treblinka II and the gas chambers. Along with my parents, Abe and Doba, and my sister, Sarale, I lost my six youngest brothers: David, Banish, Beryl, Aaron, Simche, and Yiddle. Two other brothers, Yakov-Hirsh and Usher, were also selected for liquidation, but I spontaneously grabbed them and threw them into line in back of me. There was no time to think about whether this was the right decision. My father saw what I had done for my brothers, pulling them into the line for work and life.

The *kapo* in charge noticed that there were two extra men in the detail of 150, but the Gestapo waived off his objection by saying, "What does it matter." Luckily, my brothers were not immediately thrown into the other line for being underage. Everyone else from Siemiatycze on that transport was taken to Treblinka's "shower rooms." In my dreams I still hear the agonized cries of those facing the deadly gas in those crowded chambers. I often awake in a sweat, thinking about the final moments of my dear parents and siblings who joined the communities of acrid smoke pouring out of Treblinka's crematoria.

The 152 of us were taken by train to the nearby Treblinka I complex. I shall never forget the neighbors and townsmen who shared those days with me and my brothers. They included: Abe Krawiec and his two sons; Shie Nieplotnik and his brother Shepsel; the Doliner brothers—Usher, Yankel, and Nuske; Meyer Pinchesowitz; Benzyl Trach; Abe Chaniak; Pesach Zonenfeld and his brother Kive; Mr. Lonchik the accountant; the Leff brothers, Moishe and Haim; Mr. London the pharmacist; Barbanel the electrician; Haim Weiner and Haim Akam; Benjamin Rock and his brother Abe; Gavriel the butcher; Idel Chimick; Maniek Blumenfield; Itzel Leifer; a fellow named Oleg; Soimele Farber; and Pinchus Pruss and his two sons.

Our detachment was surprised to meet a Jewish *kapo*. His name was Ben-Zion Krushewsky. He was about fifty years old and said he was from a Polish town called Falenica. As chief *kapo* of our work detail he dressed well, sporting shiny boots like the Gestapo. This former grocer had a son named Alex and a son-in-law named Joshua, both of whom he looked after in the deadly world of Treblinka I. Another *kapo* with permission to protect a relative was a man named Richter, whose nine-year-old son helped out in the kitchen. Richter even traveled on behalf of the Gestapo, and at such times it was understood that his son served as a hostage, keeping Richter from considering escape. A third *kapo* was a former banker named Ignac.

The resident Gestapo officer was Unterscharführer Preify. Herr Preify and his staff of *kapos* greeted us at our barracks by making us throw all our belongings down on a sheet spread before the front door. Anyone who did not immediately surrender all gold, jewelry, money, and weapons would be shot on the spot. Despite Krushewsky's orders not everyone complied. Haim Radzinsky's son was standing beside me and he whispered that he had a lot of money hidden in his clothes.

"What would you do in my case?" he asked. "Should I turn everything over to them?"

"No!" I responded. "That money might save your life."

"But they'll kill me if they discover it."

"What do you think they plan on doing to us here?" I said.

The young man stood firm and took my advice.

After this act of official robbery we were herded to the barracks marked with the letter C. We slept on double-decker bunks made of raw wood; we did not have even a single sheet or piece of straw. The bottom level of each bunk held thirteen men, the top level twelve. It was clear that our bodies would soon be as broken as our hearts. My brothers and I huddled together on the lower level of our bunk, no longer able to hold back our bitter tears. Only hours before we had been a large, warm family. Now we were three orphans facing almost certain doom. As we embraced tightly in the room thick with misery, Yakov-Hirsh said that we should try to survive so that one day we would be able to tell the world about the atrocities afflicted upon the Jews.

Toward evening we were joined by a group of men returning from work in the nearby town of Malkinia. It was reassuring to join them in afternoon prayer and moving to say the Kaddish for our lost families. Who would have thought that my brothers and I would be saying the Kaddish not only for our parents but also for our younger siblings? And who would say this prayer when our turn came to perish? Our murdered families had no tombstones. There was only the pervasive stench of burning flesh that wafted over the camp from the crematoria chimneys. The only sight of our loved ones was in the lazy smoke drifting heavenward above the furnaces.

To postpone our own deaths we were given watered-down imitation coffee. Soon the nine o'clock curfew arrived and no one was allowed out of the barracks. Only minutes later my townsman Eli Krawiec had to urinate and tried to go out through the door. He was shot on the spot. We saw how cheap human life was in Treblinka and how soon our Siemiatycze contingent would dwindle in size.

November 9, 1942, was our first full day at Treblinka. Our group was split into two work details to carry sand for the laying of railroad track. We were supervised by Unterscharführer Schwartz, born in Budapest, and his Ukrainian lackey Washka Olshanikow. Schwartz took an instant disliking to one of our boys—Soimele Farber, a bright, well-educated, and well-respected young man from Siemiatycze. Always impeccably dressed, this likable fellow wore a genial smile on his face. Schwartz must have bristled at the sight of this obviously superior person because he called him over and summarily struck him over the head several times with one of his clubs.

Soimele fell to the ground in a pool of blood. As soon as they could, Shepsel Nieplotnik and Barbanel the electrician rushed over to him with some water. They knew that only work would save the victim and the rest of us, so they pleaded with Soimele to get back on his feet. The poor fellow could not stand, and Schwartz returned at noon to beat him again. After work we carried Soimele onto the train back to camp and tried to return him to our barracks. But the rules did not allow him anything but a slow death. He was placed in a wired-off area designated for beating victims, and there Olshanikow beat the last few breaths out of poor Soimele. And so our detachment lost its second man.

On Tuesday, November 10, our detail returned to labor at the railroad site. This time Schwartz selected Barbanel as the object of his sadism. He struck the man several times over the head until the electrician passed out. The *Unterscharführer* loved to watch his victims suffer before they died, and Barbanel did not even last long enough for us to carry him back to camp.

When we appeared for Wednesday morning's roll call we saw numerous corpses lying on the ground near our barracks. We now realized that mortality at Treblinka I was not dependent on one overseer's sadism. That same day, November 11, a German officer killed Nuske

Doliner, the youngest of the three brothers. The next day Schwartz felled the fifth victim from our group, Simhale Pruss. With these men killed on the job it became clear that we were less than expendable. Realizing that we were not long for this world, all of us from Siemiatycze began to have desperate thoughts.

To Escape Treblinka

The first two men from our group to plot an escape were a pair of brothers-in-law who had worked together in a butcher shop and were good friends. Idel Chimick and Gavriel the butcher had once shared a house, and now these able businessmen shared a daring plot. After careful consideration they decided to burrow into the hardware store-room, where they had arranged a hiding place among the pieces of wood. They had worked out a way to break out of the camp from there.

When the two men failed to turn up for a late afternoon roll call, the *kapo* immediately reported them missing. The Gestapo informed the *lager kapo* of our barracks that 100 prisoners would be killed if the two were not found. All the *kapos* energetically hunted for the men, and a *kapo* named Alex Walnowitz found them in the supply shed. Of course, they were summarily shot in front of our assembled group.

Though intimidating, the execution did not deter the men of Siemiatycze from attempting another escape. I was part of a secret group that planned a revolt. The others included Meyer Pinchesowitz, Lonchik the accountant, Usher Doliner, Shie Nieplotnik, and Shie's brother Shepsel. Yankel Doliner was the leader of the revolt because of his organizational experience as secretary of the Zionist organization

Hashomer Hatzair.* It appeared, however, that our plan had been foiled when our work detail was broken up and some of us were sent to another part of Malkinia.

On Tuesday, November 17, the two contingents from Siemiatycze were reunited at a single work site. Our conspiracy was revived. The other section of our detail, called the Kiss grube, joined the section of which I was a member, loading wagons with sand to be shipped to the Russian front. Yankel told us to stay close to the four Ukrainian supervisors, who carried whistles to attract the immediate attention of the Germans. We would have to kill the armed guards instantaneously but quietly, preferably with an iron bar. We intended to make our move at the moment when the wagons headed out for the Russian front. The members of the revolt would then jump into the wagons, bury themselves in the sand, and wait for nightfall, climbing out when the wagons had cleared the camp compound.

Our plan was ruined by a failure of the most important element—secrecy. We knew we could trust only each other. The temptation to inform on fellow prisoners was great, because informers were often rewarded with extra food, easier jobs, and life itself. As soon as an outsider got wind of our plan, therefore, we had to postpone it until the potential betrayer was out of the way.

Beginning the following Tuesday, November 24, we lost many men from Siemiatycze within a few days. The first to go was Haim Akam. A Betarist,† he removed his coat in an open act of defiance and screamed, "I refuse to work for the murderers of my mother and father!" We all shared his sentiments but did not dare express them. As expected, Unterscharführer Shtumpe immediately had Haim shot. The next morning Maniek Blumenfield stumbled over to our barracks. "I am starving to death. Get me a piece of bread," he moaned. He collapsed and died right there on our threshold.

Our next losses could not have been more personal. My own brothers, Yakov-Hirsh and Usher, were taken to the camp gate, where they were savagely beaten to death with an iron bar. Gone was our dream of surviving the war together. I had often told them to try to be chosen for work at Malkinia. With its railroad yard Malkinia offered a chance

* See the note on pp. 10–11.
† See the note on pp. 10–11.

to jump aboard a boxcar and travel far from Treblinka to safety. I had always urged them to seize any opportunity for escape that might arise. I told them if they ever broke free they should make their way to the village of Lopusze, where a farmer and friend of our family named Boleslaw Lapusky would hide them. I promised them that I would soon join them there if they escaped before me.

I asked a *kapo* from the third block, a man named Marmurstein, to put my brothers in a detail that worked in Malkinia, and he exchanged them for two other inmates. I had said good-bye to my brothers that morning, hoping they would succeed in breaking out. Instead, they came back to the barracks filthy, tired, and thirsty from this more grueling work. I had only made things worse for them. "Why didn't you try to sneak onto a train?" I asked them in anguish. They said they could not, that they were not brave enough to try. I begged Marmurstein to return them to their easier chores closer to the barracks. He said he would do so but that it would take some time to accomplish. Within the week my brothers, may their souls rest in peace, had been killed.

The loss really struck me when I returned to the barracks from work. I had had to be strong for them. I had been like a father to them. Now that they had "escaped" from Treblinka in the usual way, I wondered if, indeed, I would soon join them. I cried like a child. I felt responsible for their deaths because they would not have gone outside the camp to work if I had not urged them to go to Malkinia to attempt an escape. I had never allowed them to join me in any work detail so that if an entire detail were killed at least one of us would survive. Now I was the family's only chance.

My brothers live on in the faces of my two sons, David and John, who bear a remarkable likeness to Usher and Yakov-Hirsh. They also share the same Hebrew names. In fact, in one of our last conversations my brothers and I swore that if any of us survived, and if a world with normal people again existed, we would name our children for the ones we lost.

The inevitability of death in Treblinka did not soften the blow for me. It was horrifying enough to hear how my parents had perished in the gas chambers, but now I had to live with the knowledge that my brothers had been beaten to death by inhuman hooligans.

In my agony, my instinct for survival etched the physical description of Treblinka I deep in my memory. The workday began at the barracks, the second section of which served as a storage shed. All the shovels, hammers, and other tools used for each day's work were carefully dispensed by our designated supervisor, a man named Majorek. Each tool and quantity of material were accounted for. At the end of every working day every tool had to be signed back in. There was no opportunity to hide tools for use in a nighttime revolt.

Stationed at the other end of the barracks were skilled laborers such as blacksmiths, welders, carpenters, and locksmiths. I worked mostly with this group as an oven specialist. My experience with ovens allowed me to repair and maintain the small heating ovens used by the Gestapo and other Germans. The most remarkable members of the skilled-labor group were the Jewish carpenters from the nearby town of Kosów. These five carpenters had built Treblinka from scratch. Their families were protected, and these men were allowed to go home every Friday and return every Sunday afternoon. During the week they lived in a separate barracks with other carpenters. Barracks C, unlike Barracks B, in which they lived, was never given special privileges but instead was always singled out for the sadistic whims of our captors.

One barracks to which none of us wanted to transfer was the quarantine bloc. By no stretch of the imagination did that barracks constitute a hospital or clinic. Rather, it was a vestibule to the crematorium. No one stayed there for more than a few days without being put out of his misery. But hunger, exposure, and fatigue caught up with many of us, and I too soon found myself dragged to this building that few left on their feet.

One Friday night I came down with a high fever. My situation was critical, but medicine was not to be wasted on Jews. Fortunately, the doctor in charge when I arrived was Dr. Katzenellenbogen from my hometown of Siemiatycze. He told me I had typhus. Knowing me well, he stayed up with me all night applying cold compresses. He knew I would not survive without special care.

That night in my fevered state I dreamed that my mother visited me. We were in a slaughterhouse full of stinking bodies. My mother ran away to some distant fields and I lost sight of her. The doctor told me the next morning that I had talked in my sleep for most of that crucial night. As expected, Unterscharführers Lindiken and Shtumpe came into the quarantine bloc to clear it out. They shouted for everyone to step outside into the cold. Things would get colder still for those who could not move. Like G-d's protecting angel, the Jewish *lager kapo,* Ignac, came by and pointed me out to the Germans.

"That man is our oven specialist. He knows his profession very well. He fixes all the ovens that heat your barracks. If you kill him we have no one suitable to replace him."

Lindiken asked the doctor what this oven man's diagnosis was, and Dr. Katzenellenbogen said that I had a bad case of the flu. He predicted that I would return to work in two or three days at the most. The Germans ordered me to get back in bed while they dragged the other poor souls out into the cold. A Mr. Pinkus, whose bed was near mine, handed me fifty Polish zlotys and a stash of bread he'd been keeping. I wanted to refuse so precious a gift as bread, but he insisted with a terrible urgency.

"Take it! I won't have any use for it anymore. They are going to take me out and kill me in a moment."

We both knew he was right, and this was the only way to keep this treasure from the body searchers. At least half of the patients were too weak to complain about their imminent deaths, or else they welcomed them as a relief from their suffering. The others became animated with the sudden courage of those facing certain death. As they were dragged naked into the freezing January cold they loudly cursed the Germans and spit on them. Marked for torture and certain death, they now had nothing to lose. This was the Saturday morning routine of clearing out the infirmary.

Following my miraculous reprieve, I recovered enough to return to my job of maintaining the heating ovens. After the deathly confines of the infirmary I was relieved to be back in the three-kilometer-square world of the labor *lager.* Roll call for Barracks B and C roused us at 6:00 A.M. Two or three feeding times punctuated each day, with meals consisting of imitation coffee in the morning, a late afternoon bowl of watery carrot and potato soup (with, at most, a drop of grain, and all of the vegetables taken by the more privileged), and an evening banquet of 100 grams of bread.

Kapo Krushewsky distributed food to my subgroup of twenty-four. The entire block had to pull together because we would all be killed if any one of us attempted to do anything like escape. The men in my group came back to the barracks at around 7:00 P.M., dirty, tired, and hungry from an entire day of loading heavy coil in Malkinia. Our first priority was to smuggle in some food to keep these walking skeletons alive and our group intact. We had some former butchers in our barracks, and on a couple of occasions they managed to obtain part of a dead horse from the Germans, expertly prepare it, and serve it in our soup. Horse meat is not kosher, but the rare infusion of protein surely kept some of us alive.

Our source of drinking and cooking water was a well near Barracks C. Sadly, this well served as a source of death too. Many a broken prisoner jumped in head first to end his suffering by drowning himself. The rest of us were dying even more slowly and in greater agony, the lice gnawing at us no less than the hunger. There was nothing we could do to prevent our barracks from being infested with these voracious creatures that tormented us at a time when we needed every precious moment of sleep. One night I was awakened by a particularly large invasion of these demons crawling over my face and body. I looked up to see that the man in the bunk above me was stripping his body of lice and throwing them down on me.

I was always careful not to vent my rage at the Nazis on my fellow prisoners. But now this man from Grodno was testing my patience. I yelled at him to throw his lice on the floor; I had more than I needed right now. When he continued to drop lice near me I threatened him with my shoe. I finally got through to him, but a few days later I had more trouble from him. Cold urine spilled down from the bunk above. Too ill to get down to use the latrine, he was using a bottle, which began to overflow. For the first time during my stay in hell I was dehumanized to such an extent that I wished for this bunkmate to be removed in the next Saturday night selection. Our captors did not disappoint me.

Krushewsky presided over the weekly selections by the sixty-five-year-old Unterscharführer Preify. Each week between 50 and 100 men were taken to Treblinka II, to the gas chambers. Each new transport of Jews brought healthy young slaves, so why not throw the old ones into the ovens to make way for the new, equally expendable crop? The number of men removed from our group varied each week, so we never knew what to expect.

One day the Gestapo sent 100 men to the work station at Malkinia. There at the railroad yard they worked hard to gain another day of life from their German overlords and from their *kapo,* a man named Paff, who was from the town of Węgrów. Although there was no indication that they had not done their work well enough, they were transported to Treblinka II. Instead of returning to their barracks, they went to the crematoria.

When the Ukrainian guards returned to Barracks C without the prisoners, our *kapos* asked them what had happened to the Jews. The Ukrainian guards smiled and pointed at the black smoke pouring out of the chimneys. All those men, alive that morning, had already gone up in smoke. There were too many newer, younger, healthier men to replace them, and so they were terminated with the finality of Treblinka.

Kapo Paff was visibly shaken and had obviously not been involved in the decision. In our world he was definitely one of the good ones. There were more than enough sadists, like Unterscharführer Lanz. I once observed him at work from a window of the locksmith's room where I was assigned. He went over to a Jewish prisoner and asked him his name. The response was "Daitch, from Berlin." For no apparent reason Lanz struck him with his truncheon, continuing to beat the poor man until he was dead.

At roll call the next morning, a Saturday, Lanz asked for carpenters. About twenty hands went up, including those of Abe and Benjamin Horowitz, whom I knew from Siemiatycze. Signed up as a work unit, the carpenters went that Monday morning with Lanz, Preify, and a half dozen Ukrainian guards to the village of Starowies. They did not return for a week. When they did we discovered that they had lived in army barracks and received the most precious compensation we could imagine—near normal amounts of food. The mere thought of a buttered piece of bread could drive one to distraction.

This paradise lasted three weeks, at the end of which the contingent was ordered to dismantle the army barracks they had slept in. After they completed this last task they were marched back to Barracks C, lined up, and shot.

Somehow the lives of workers in Treblinka I became even more expendable. A particularly bad reign of terror began with a heavy snow-fall on March 22 or 23, 1943. The Germans ordered us to remove the snow outside the barracks. A Nazi was posted at our only door with an ax and several vicious dogs. He would arbitrarily swing the ax at the heads of prisoners, trying to lop them off in one swipe. In that hellish week dozens of inmates fell to sickness, bullets, and that brutal ax. As death closed its jaws around us, most of us became paralyzed with terror and despair. A few, myself among them, resolved to escape.

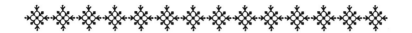

Working the Road to Survival

$\mathcal{M}$arch had begun with a transport of Jews from Grodno. When I reported for my usual job I was told that I was being replaced by a new man. This meant only one thing in Treblinka—death. I was crushed, but also angry. If I expressed my bitterness I would be killed on the spot, so I decided to appeal to the good Mr. Majorek, who was in charge of the toolshed. I told him what had happened to me and reminded him that I was a knowledgeable veteran. Having survived Treblinka since November 1942, I had unbelievable seniority. I knew every moment of his daily routine of issuing and checking in tools from each *kapo's* work group. He could not promise me anything, but I did stay with him that perilous Friday when I had no life-giving assignment.

At Saturday morning roll call Rottenführer Wise and Niecheslaw Hochko, a Jewish *kapo*, asked who in our group knew how to build a road. My arm shot up. I said that I had much experience building roads. When this statement was challenged, I listed the tools I would need for the job. I mentioned a builder's level, ropes to mark off the parameters, picks, shovels, and wheelbarrows for moving earth. My imagination saved my life, and I was placed at the head of a twenty-four-man contingent of road builders.

The supervisors and I worked out a routine of measuring and digging out a foundation, straightening the roadbed, laying down flagstone and curbstones, and making sure that rainwater would drain to the curbs. I overheard Rottenführer Wise complimenting us *Wegebavers* (road builders) to Hochko. He was apparently quite impressed—and would have been all the more so if he had known that I had no road-building experience. His approval of our work meant nothing less than survival.

One morning at roll call Kapo Krushewsky received an order to send 100 men to Treblinka II and the gas chambers. All 500 of us in the barracks knew that this could be our final call. Among the unlucky ones was a townsman of mine named Shie Shewc. His brother, a professional electrician who worked in the power station in Treblinka I, tried to beg Unterscharführer Preify for mercy. But Treblinka had no ears or heart for appeals. Numbers ruled, numbers of faceless victims brought in by train and brought out through the chimney.

Not only the relatives of valuable workers lacked protection. Even the professional inmates could not avoid being chosen. At the same selection a dentist was called to take his inevitable place in Treblinka II. The dentist begged Kapo Ignac for mercy, since Ignac was a close friend of his mother, who worked on the laundry detail in Milawko. Ignac responded not with a blow but with a bow to Jewish law: "If your name comes up I cannot substitute another man to die in your place. I would then be a murderer. I am not allowed to judge who shall live and who shall die. I have my orders, and I dare not interfere for personal reasons." Unconsoled, we suffered the loss of two more precious souls from Siemiatycze.

One day soon afterward the SS ordered us to transport several tons of sand. Joining our group was a man named Wolchik from the Grodno transport, an older man who could not work as hard as the Germans expected. I tried to cover for him by working harder on my side of the wheelbarrow. An SS man saw Wolchik struggling to do his part, so he threw him to the ground and beat him. He died the next day from his wounds.

As hard as I was working, I too received some twenty blows to the head and body from an overseer's shovel. If I had lost my balance or composure I would have died from these cruelties, which left me bruised and swollen. Later I used some of my fake coffee in a compress to relieve the painful welts. I put the failed escape plans of the past behind me and sought new ways to consider escape.

During our road building, supervised by Kapo Hochko, a nearby forest caught my eye. If only I could reach those trees I might escape from the vicinity of Treblinka that very night. With nothing to lose I boldly approached Hochko and whispered to him, as I worked, that the forest could be our path to freedom. He struck me on the head and back and called me a big talker, but he also told me he would speak to me later. When my job of removing stones brought us together again, I whispered that I had put my life in his hands by sharing this plan with him. Hochko struck me more softly this time and made it clear that he was hitting me to cover up our conversation from the Ukrainian guard, who had already lifted his rifle to shoot me.

"It's OK, don't shoot the bastard," Hochko called to the guard. "I'm only hitting him because he is young enough to work faster than he is. Rottenführer Wise wants this road completed right away, and we must pick up the pace."

That evening Hochko called me over to a corner outside the barracks. "You have some kind of guts to talk such nonsense to a *kapo*. Maybe we can work something out."

We arranged to meet the next night at the same time and place. We agreed that if we spoke at the work place he would scream at me and hit me as a cover. I swore to him that I would never betray anyone who confided in me, even under torture. The *kapo* clearly knew that his own life hung by a thread here at Treblinka and that this might be his last slim chance for survival.

The next evening Hochko told me that an escape from the road-building site was possible, though it would entail great risk and require drastic actions and more men. He would have to effect a turnover of men in our work detail, bringing in an underworld element that could be trusted to pull off a complex maneuver with daring and precision. We must attempt to break out without firing a single shot. Gunfire or violence would doom our escape by provoking an immediate and massive response from the Ukrainian guards and German soldiers.

In the days ahead I was given brief messages to convey to several men I had not known previously. I was strictly forbidden to elaborate on any information. If asked, I was to deny being a leader of the conspiracy and to deny knowing who was planning the escape. I was to stay as far as possible from Hochko. And so it was that I met the likes of Leon and Stefan, robbers from Warsaw, and Jacob and Motty, horse thieves from Sokołów Podlaski. I also spoke with Yalowiec, a chemical engineer, and other specialists named Pavel, Shmulik, Prawda, and Moniek.

Hochko told Rottenführer Wise that he needed men with better training for his road-building detail. However, the thirteen or so men he brought in were really chosen for their ability to be resourceful in a desperate situation. They were more likely to be skilled at killing a man quietly and quickly with a length of wire than at leveling a roadbed. Wise instructed Krushewsky, now an *oberkapo,* to approve Hochko's personnel changes, but Krushewsky suspected that something was up. He placed his own son Alex on our work detail to see what Hochko and his criminals were up to. The fifteen of us co-conspirators were on alert to say nothing in Alex's presence. When the spy asked me what it was that people were whispering, all I said to him was, "Please get me something to eat; I'm so very hungry."

Alex reported to his father that I was a hardworking idiot. If something was afoot, he said, I was apparently oblivious to it. Alex the spy was truly in the dark, so his frustrated father withdrew him from our unit after a couple of weeks. With Krushewsky's suspicions abated, we resumed planning our escape.

My hunger almost cost me my life when my job gathering stones brought me close to a stable. The Germans kept various animals there, including pigs for eating and dogs for tearing up prisoners. A Jew named Shmuel Dovid, whose job it was to feed the animals, was boiling potatoes for the pigs. The smell of food made me do something desperate. I dug a small hole and waited for a chance to run in and take some potatoes. I planned to hide them in the hole and eat them when no one was watching. After a while Shmuel Dovid did leave the potato pot to cool. Without thinking twice I ran in, grabbed some potatoes, and tossed them into the hole. I covered them with some stones and went back to work.

When Shmuel Dovid returned he noticed that some potatoes were missing and angrily accused me of taking them. I told him I had not the slightest idea what he was talking about, but he did not let the matter rest. He made a scene and threatened to go to Rottenführer Wise. This meant that I would probably lose my new potatoes as well as my life.

Fortunately, Shmuel Dovid was appeased by one of our older workers, a man from the town of Kosów who worked with his son. He told Shmuel Dovid, "Calm down. Don't waste your time. Just boil some more potatoes and forget about it. People who don't work with animals can't get food like you can. The rest of us are starving to death. And besides, who is to say that you will not be killed for allowing the potatoes to be taken? How many lives should be lost over a handful of pig food?"

Shmuel Dovid still insisted on checking my hands and pockets. He found nothing incriminating. He even asked Hochko if he knew who had taken his potatoes. Hochko came through and covered up for me, so Shmuel Dovid finally let the matter rest.

When the injured party was gone, I uncovered the boiled potatoes and shared them with Hochko and several others who had come to my aid. We had ourselves a feast, but it had nearly been the most expensive meal of my life.

Around this time the SS decided that they were not employing enough sadism in destroying our bodies and souls at Treblinka. They were especially concerned that they were murdering the patients in quarantine much too quickly without deriving the proper amount of sick pleasure from their deeds. War is no time to pass up on good entertainment, so they decided to employ a steamroller in an ingenious new way. Unterscharführer Preify divided twenty men from Barracks C into two groups of ten. He then ordered Kapo Krushewsky to take the sick men out of the infirmary. Each group of ten workers was harnessed with heavy ropes to a large wheeled machine, while the sick men were tied between the heavy wheels, which were joined by a thick iron axle.

The Germans beat the healthy men at the wheels, forcing them to mangle the sick men in the middle. When the Nazis tired of driving this torture machine, they handed the whips to their eager Ukrainian lackeys. No schoolboy torturing frogs ever had more fun than these inhuman supermen were having as they mocked and teased their helpless victims with endless delight.

When the bloody orgy ended, dozens of half-dead Jews were left to die in the customary spot between the two gates. Then their bodies were disposed of like garbage, tossed into a ravine in the nearby woods.

The corpses were covered with more corpses and half-corpses (some unfortunates still clung to life) along with a thin layer of earth. Groups of men, like my own, now had to worry as they returned from work about being forced to participate in "the last dance"—the name for the *Hauptsturmführer's* new amusement with the steamroller. This was a new worry on top of our concern that any work detail might be shipped to the gas chambers of Treblinka II rather than returned to its barracks in Treblinka I.

Occasionally the Ukrainian guards, men who so loved their work at Treblinka that they volunteered for it, would show that they too could torture helpless Jews. When a work contingent returned tired and dirty from a day's slave labor, they would, on the coldest days, force the Jews to strip outside and take an ice-cold shower.

As much as the Ukrainians tried to show their equal status to the Nazis, nothing could compare to the cultured and civilized way that the Germans displayed barbarity. On May 1, 1943, Unterscharführer Preify wanted to celebrate German victories on the Russian front with a big party. Because none of the Germans were capable of playing a musical instrument with any skill, they searched among the Jewish prisoners for a good musician. Kapo Krushewsky easily found one, a distinguished professor of music who was a first-class violinist. As the Germans feasted into the early morning hours, the poor musician was forced to play incessantly from the high guard tower. To reward the professor for all the gaiety he provided, the Nazis threw him to his death from the tower.

Despite the numbing hunger, brutality, and fear, the prisoners at Treblinka II carried out an uprising in August 1943.* Many prisoners tried to escape at once, too many for the machine guns, barriers, and dogs to stop them all. Some escaping inmates made it to the woods near our road-building site, and our first instinct was to act on our own escape plans then and there. Our armed guards were on the alert, however, and it would have been suicidal to try anything just then.

Reduced to spectators, we rooted for a group of escapees who suc-

---

* The famous uprising at Treblinka, which had been planned for months, took place on August 2. Some 750 inmates were killed as they tried to escape; only 70 escapees survived. The rebels succeeded in killing several guards and burning most of the camp to the ground.

cessfully eluded their pursuers. The SS did catch up to one woman from that group, dragging her back to the camp. The Germans publicly punished her for deserting their extermination factory by hanging her from a pole by her feet. Kapo Hochko commented that the Germans could not allow her the decency or luxury of a quick death. It was clear to all of us what lay in store for those who were caught trying to escape.

One morning soon after that I came down with an unbearable toothache. I tried to work but my inflamed wisdom tooth drove me to distraction. I knew that the Treblinka dentist only treated Germans and that I risked death by going to see him—yet the pain goaded me to his office.

"Go away!" the dentist ordered. "I cannot serve Jews."

"I won't leave until you help me," I replied, sitting myself down in the dentist's chair.

A German officer walked in and decided to enforce Treblinka's sense of propriety. He asked me where the pain was and I replied that it was in the wisdom tooth on my right side. I explained that the pain was preventing me from doing my work.

The Nazi ordered the dentist to remove the wisdom tooth—but from my left side. He pulled out his revolver, cocked it, and pointed it at my head. "If you make a sound, Jew, this bullet will go through your mouth."

As the dentist proceeded to pull out the healthy wisdom tooth from my left side, I clutched the sides of the chair with all my strength. The pain was incredible, but I did not cry out. The blood from my mouth ran over my clothes.

"There, Jew. How do you feel now that I have given you some dental treatment? Do you feel any more pain?"

"No, Untersturmführer. No pain at all, thank you," I said as I got up briskly and left. Watching me suffer must have given him enough pleasure because he did not shoot me on my way out. Dizzy with pain, I made my way to the toolshed to find someone who would remove my bad tooth. No lack of hygiene or technique could be worse than the Treblinka-style dentistry I had experienced.

While at Majorek's toolshed I learned something that would take my mind off my throbbing tooth. Majorek and Kapo Ignac, a fine, trustworthy fellow, were organizing an escape from Treblinka I. The toolshed would be the center of activity. Every day at 9:00 A.M. sharp Untersturm-führer Lanz came to Majorek's station to go over the day's work plan and requisition the necessary tools. The conspirators planned to strike him on the head with an iron bar as soon as he entered the shed. The blow would kill him immediately and then they would strip him of his clothing.

Ignac's build was similar to that of Lanz, so he would put on the officer's uniform. He would then approach the nearby Ukrainian guard and order him down from his observation post. Majorek and the others would kill the guard quickly and quietly. Next they would go after Rottenfüh-rer Wise, who was at the horse stable at precisely 9:00 A.M. every day.

I was entrusted with the escape plan of Hochko's group, and it was taboo to give any information to anyone who did not absolutely have to know. I had to keep secrets as though our lives depended on it, because they most certainly did. Although I was intrigued by Ignac's plan, I had to stick to my work group. The leader of our conspiracy, Hoch-ko, also concluded that now was the time to strike. We planned to kill the Ukrainian guard stationed closest to us at the post facing Treblin-ka I. Without access to a German officer's uniform, we would have to use guile to approach the guard. Hochko would attract his attention by bringing him vodka, salami, and bread that one of our men, Shloi-mele, had arranged to obtain with the help of a local peasant. The smuggled goods cost us twenty dollars in gold, but it was absolutely necessary for our first and last chance to escape.

Not all of us had the nerve required to carry out our plans. In our group was a Mr. Cigler, who had run a taxi business in Warsaw. He alarmed us all by telling Hochko that he wanted out of our conspiracy.

"Listen, Mr. Hochko, I've changed my mind. We know that if we suc-ceed many Jews will be killed in retaliation. I'm not sure I can live with that. I'm a man of sixty years. My wife and children, my whole family, have been killed. I don't think I could build a new family if I managed to es-cape. Let me report sick to Kapo Krushewsky and be taken to the infir-mary. My heart is not in it anymore, so I had better take myself out."

When Stefan, a member of our group, heard about this defection he grew alarmed. He told Hochko and Shloimele that we would have to kill Cigler along with the Ukrainian guard. Hochko would not hear of it.

"Calm down. Cigler is still an honest and noble person. You can trust him. Don't even think of doing anything so foolish. If you touch Cigler you'll be the first to die. All of you must listen to me. I trust Cigler with my life. With G-d's help we will succeed. We will be free in a matter of hours."

When we went back to the barracks for lunch Hochko kept Stefan and Shloimele from harming Cigler. Too tense to drink my bowl of soup, I brought it to my townsman Dr. Katzenellenbogen, who had helped me through my illness. If he had not kept me alive I would not have been part of this attempt to escape. The doctor thanked me and wished me luck. I wondered if he suspected we were up to something, but I dared not bring up the subject.

We returned to our assigned labor near the forest. While we worked on the roadbed Shloimele met our local contact and then brought the salami, bread, and vodka to the Ukrainian guard. As it turned out, the most precious item to us was the least interesting to him. The guard nonchalantly gave much of the bread back to the laborers and went to work on the vodka.

Hochko informed us that everything was on schedule for our escape. It was three in the afternoon, with only an hour or so of daylight left. We would make our break when darkness provided a cover. The Germans did not usually pursue fugitives at night, when the elements evened the odds for a desperate and dangerous foe.

Our Ukrainian guard was now quite drunk. Hochko positioned Stefan on the right, Shloimele on the left, and Shmulik in the middle as they slowly approached the prone guard, making sure to block the view of the guard in the watchtower. They killed the guard silently with a piece of metal. It was over very quickly. This was a chilling moment, not one we could celebrate, because we had all passed the point of no return.

Shmulik changed clothes with the guard while the rest of us hid the body from view. Our new "guard" kept a rifle trained as Hochko barked orders at us to take wheelbarrows toward the forest. One of the wheelbarrows held the body of the guard, which we dumped beneath a large tree. We followed Motty, who knew the area well, walking briskly as the sun sank. We resisted the temptation to run, continuing the pretense that we were a work detail under the careful watch of a *kapo* and an armed guard. Shmulik spoke German well and would do the talking if we encountered anyone.

Out of Treblinka

$\mathcal{A}$ farmer chopping wood nearby soon spotted us. Stefan said that we should kill the farmer so he would not send the Germans after us. But Hochko told him that killing an innocent man would accomplish nothing. In fact, Hochko went right up to the man and demanded his identification papers, which he then pocketed.

"We are a group of 200 escaped prisoners," Hochko told the frightened farmer. "If we have any trouble from the Germans we will kill you and your entire family. We know who you are. We will burn your farm to the ground."

Motty then asked the man for directions to the town we were looking for. As we started off we went in the opposite direction from the farmer's advice. We would soon know if Motty was correct in second-guessing the man. A few kilometers down the road Hochko fell to the ground. He clutched his leg in pain and could no longer walk. He had trouble with a pinched nerve and the tension of the escape must have been too much for him.

"I'm not going to leave you behind," I said to the man who engineered our escape.

"No, no, my child. Run ahead with the rest of them. Why should you die because of me? You are young. You might make it."

I could not leave him, so I lifted him onto my shoulders and carried him. We managed to catch up to the others when they stopped to rest.

Stefan, Jacob, and Pavel came over to us, but not to ask how Hochko was doing. They planned to make their way to Warsaw and wanted the rifle from Shmulik.

"We can't let you have it," said Hochko, still in charge despite his injury. "Besides, you won't need it in the city, but we will need it here."

Hochko understood that they were leaving us, and we wanted to part on good terms. I went over to shake their hands, but they declined. They said shaking hands brought bad luck. Even though they caused us some trouble, I was sorry to see these tough guys go. We lost another valuable member of our group that night when Motty disappeared. He was to have been our guide to the Kurczewsky forest where we hoped to link up with the Polish underground or a band of partisans.

Our chief enemies now were not the Germans but our stomachs. We had been without food or drink for nearly two days, since escaping from Treblinka. Only Shmulik and Hochko had the ability to confront people without arousing suspicion, so the two of them, with our one rifle, approached an isolated farmhouse.

Hochko knocked on the door and began speaking to the farmer in perfect Polish, which was his native tongue. He said that he and his men were members of the Polish underground and that the farmer should not fear his uniform or the rifle. He told the man that we had not eaten in days and needed his help to continue fighting the Germans. The farmer responded by giving Hochko and Shmulik food for themselves and the "soldiers" in the nearby woods. As "soldiers" we were armed only with sticks, but we were on the alert for anything that might go wrong.

Shmulik's leveled rifle encouraged the farmer to be generous, and we soon had some much-needed food in our bellies. We headed for the safety of the dense Kurczewsky forest, but we did not feel very secure there. Something smelled fishy; there was danger in the air. Perhaps the farmer had informed on us and we were being followed? It occurred to us that our gangster friends would probably have murdered the farmer and his family and then taken everything they had. Perhaps their way made more sense in the hellish world we lived in?

We walked for many kilometers before resting again. Hochko, now

131

limping on his own, had been thinking the whole time. He assembled everyone and addressed us.

"I want you all to listen to what I have to tell you. We must have discipline around here if we are going to survive. We must not act as individuals because we could all pay the price. Everything must be done with a plan and everyone must cooperate when orders are given. Shmulik and I must be in charge for now. We will listen to every good suggestion, however, and we will vote on anything dangerous that affects the group.

"Our biggest problem now is getting food. Until we get civilian clothes for the rest of you, Shmulik and I must be the only ones to face the Poles. The safest way for us to get food is by intercepting farmers taking wagons of food to the market. We will wait for an individual farmer, so we don't have to worry about several farmers putting up a fight."

We all listened and then approved the plan. About four o'clock the next morning we spotted a lone farmer coming down the road in a wagon. Hochko and Shmulik stood in the middle of the road and Hochko called out to him in his excellent German: "Halt! Show me your papers!"

Seeing the uniform and hearing the German orders, the intimidated farmer pulled his wagon to a complete stop. He cooperated with the interrogation, telling Hochko where he was going, where he had come from, and what he was carrying in the wagon. The farmer denied carrying contraband food for sale on the black market, but when he unloaded his wagon on the side of the road for investigation, there was bread, milk, cheese, smoked ham, salami, bacon, and even water.

Hochko ordered the farmer to appear at German police headquarters at nine o'clock the next morning to pay a fine of 200 Reichmarks. He would then have his documents returned to him. If he failed to appear promptly, the police would come to him. And this, Hochko assured him, would prove to be a most unpleasant experience.

The farmer probably felt he was getting off easy as he turned his wagon around and started back the way he had come. When he was out of sight we picked up the precious food and divided it among ourselves in the safety of the forest. Hochko warned us that our stomachs, starved for so long, would not be able to digest a large quantity of rich food at one time. He advised us to eat slowly and in small quantities no matter what our eyes and stomachs seemed to say.

Although our experiences along this road had been rewarding, we realized that we had to move away to avoid investigation by the Poles or Germans. With so many members of our group having gone off on their own, the authorities had certainly been informed by now about the Treblinka escapees and had probably sent out search parties to look for us.

As we walked, Shloimele challenged Hochko for the rifle that Hochko had been holding. Shloimele assured us that he would get plenty of food for the five of us who remained together, but Hochko categorically refused to give him the gun. Shloimele was a street-smart thug but one we could trust. Hochko knew that Shloimele's efforts would bring results, but he was concerned about his methods. On the other extreme was Yalowiec. From a well-educated and wealthy home, Yalowiec thought he could appeal to a farmer's finer instincts and get food by earnest solicitation. Shloimele sneered at this suggestion, saying that he knew the Polish people much better and that force was the only way to get anything from them.

Yalowiec did try to get some food for us, but he returned from his mission tired and empty-handed. Shloimele crowed about his superior knowledge and skills but could not get the rifle from Hochko for a foray of his own. "Rifle or not," Shloimele proclaimed, "I will show you how I can provide you some food."

Shloimele left us around noon and made his way to a farmhouse. Boldly he looked through the windows and then went right in. He headed straight for the hearth, knowing that farmers often smoked meat by hanging it several feet up their chimneys. Sure enough, he found armfuls of meat. He filled a sack with bread and ham. He saw a pot of soup on the stove ready for the family's lunch and poured it into a pail. He even took knives, forks, and dishes. Heavily laden, Shloimele made his way back to us in the forest. He certainly earned his bragging rights.

We did not get a chance to enjoy this banquet at our leisure, however, because we suddenly heard a fusillade of German automatic weapon fire spraying the woods and coming toward us. The furious farmer must have gone right to the Nazi authorities. Hochko told us not to panic but to crawl away from the advancing fire. With only one rifle we would have no chance in a fight. They did not know exactly where we were, but they clearly hoped to draw return fire or to flush us out. The Germans would only shoot from the periphery of the forest, since they were deathly afraid of confrontations with wily partisans.

We kept moving for a few days, covering our trail and staying out of range of their firing. They attempted one massive assault but guessed wrong about our location. In all the confusion and movement we lost both Hochko and Shmulik. We tried to make contact with them but could not. That left three of us, Yalowiec, Shloimele, and me. Each of us wanted to split up and go to his hometown. Yalowiec wanted to return to Grodno, and I thought my chances of survival were best in the familiar villages around my native Siemiatycze.

Each of us had to stay within sight of the Bug River to reach our destination. Because the river was the border between occupied German territory and a German protectorate,* there were patrols of German border guards to watch out for. The three of us were by the river at around two in the afternoon, on a sunny Sunday in September 1943, when danger descended on us in a hurry.

Two German soldiers patrolling in a horse cart were heading our way. We had only a few moments to get out of their sight. We decided to crawl under a small bridge we had passed earlier. The Germans were heading right for the bridge and we heard them singing a song. It was a song about the war soon coming to an end and Germany being free of Jews. Little did they know that as they sang they were a few feet away from three Jews who had escaped from death's jaws.

We crouched uncomfortably under that small bridge for at least an hour before deciding to walk along the river to find a safe way across. We knew the bridge was constantly patrolled. We thought it would be possible to swim across at night, but Shloimele could not swim. As we searched for a rowboat or raft, a fifteen-year-old boy spotted us. He had his own troubles, however, and did not seem anxious to report some suspicious walking skeletons who had probably come from a prison camp. Some of the cows he was herding were drowning in the river, and we waded to help. The boy showed his gratitude by responding fully to Yalowiec's questions about the river. This local expert knew where we

---

* See the note on p. 9.

could best cross the Bug and what we could expect on the opposite bank. As the boy pointed to some tall bushes on the other side I recognized the village there as one near Siemiatycze. This familiar place was where I should go.

Yalowiec gave the boy a beautiful carving knife in exchange for leading Shloimele across the river. The boy knew where Shloimele could wade across without having to swim. Yalowiec and I swam to join up with Shloimele. We had just arrived at the opposite bank when an old woman from the nearby village signaled to us that a patrol was approaching. We dove into some tall bushes as a carriage full of Germans passed by. We now knew that both banks of the river were full of soldiers. We stayed in the bushes long enough to determine the frequency of the patrols so we could remove our wet clothes and dry them in the sun.

At one point we had no time to retrieve our shirts without being spotted by a German patrol. We had to think fast or perish. In front of us in a large field were several rakes lying beside large clumps of hay. It was a Sunday afternoon so none of the local farmers were at work. We grabbed the rakes and began to work hard gathering hay as the German patrol passed. We did not turn around, as if we were used to passing patrols. Luckily, they did not say a word either, so accustomed to seeing shirtless laborers in the field that they forgot it was Sunday. Can you imagine what would have happened if they had realized that they had just passed a trio of Jews—escapees from Treblinka at that?

When the patrol was out of sight we walked through the field, reasoning that the German presence would thin out as we moved farther from the river. We were soon met by a well-dressed man whom I thought must be the *soltis* (head) of the village. This turned out to be the case, and the field we were on belonged to him. Not at all hostile, he displayed genuine concern for our safety in this heavily patrolled area.

"You are in a border area," he explained to us. "Walking around in broad daylight makes you an easy target."

Yalowiec, with his perfect aristocratic Polish, did the talking. "We are honored to make your acquaintance, kind sir. As you may know, the Yalowiec family is one of the leading families in the city of Grodno. If you would be gracious enough to hide us for the duration of the war, I will sign over to you some of the best properties in the city. It will be a pleasure for me to make you a wealthy man."

"Your offer is generous, but I'm afraid my home is too dangerous a place. The Germans are constantly in and out of my house. My daughters and I have our hands full entertaining German officers. I shall give you a roof for tonight and bring you some food. But early tomorrow morning you must leave. It is best for all of us."

The village official was true to his word. We slept in a barn and were brought bread, butter, and warm milk. We also received directions to our respective destinations, Yalowiec and Shloimele to Grodno, and I to the village of Lopusze. I only had to travel a distance of twelve kilometers, but I would be going alone. Shloimele had made up his mind to travel with Yalowiec, banking for survival on the intelligence and poise of his wealthy friend. To enable Yalowiec to do all the talking in his superior Polish, Shloimele planned to pretend to be mute and to feign injury by wearing a bandage over one eye. I myself spoke Polish with a Yiddish inflection, but I planned to depend on Polish acquaintances from before the war.

Early the next morning we parted company. We shook hands and wished each other G-d's help in surviving the war. "*Zayt matsliakh,*" they said, wishing me luck as I turned alone toward the village of Lopusze.

I had been walking for an hour when I encountered a man I recognized from Siemiatycze. He was amazed to see me and came over for a closer look.

"Why are you walking around like this in broad daylight?" he asked me. "The Germans are sure to kill you this way."

"I escaped from the death camp of Treblinka," I explained.

"You think you have escaped death? You are headed right for a death trap. There is a German checkpoint at the town of Drohiczyn nad Bugiem. They'll shoot you on the spot as soon as they see you. You had better take a different road to Lopusze."

The man told me how to get to Lopusze and avoid the Germans. He also inquired after my family, having known my parents, brothers, and little sister. I told him that two of my brothers had been beaten to death and the others had been killed in the gas chambers and burned to ashes at Treblinka. I thanked him for his invaluable information and made my way to the home of Boleslaw Lapusky.

I was much closer to Lapusky than I was to the man I had met earlier, so when he asked me about my family I broke down and cried. When I regained my composure I told him that my family had all been killed at Treblinka. I told him that I had seen with my own eyes the smoke rising from the crematoria chimneys when my mother's, father's, brothers', and sister's bodies were burned. A sensitive man, Lapusky too broke down and cried. He could not believe that such atrocities could be committed against innocent men, women, and children. He could not understand how human beings could become such animals.

I assured him everything was true, that I was an eyewitness. I explained that thousands of Jews were killed every day in the huge and orderly slaughterhouse named Treblinka. I described the layouts and functions of Treblinka I and Treblinka II and told him of the volunteers who helped the murderers by eagerly torturing Jews before they killed them in this immense factory of death.

Lapusky told me that my mother was the finest and most intelligent person he had ever met. I thanked him for his kind words and hoped he would be receptive to the question that I had walked so far to ask . . . the question that during my eternity in Treblinka I dreamed I would one day ask him: "May I hide here in your stable from the Germans?"

He told me I could stay only one night. Fortunately the one night was stretched on a daily basis to two weeks. While not physically uncomfortable, these two weeks were devastating emotionally. Now that I no longer had to expend all my energy on survival, I had time to remember what had happened to me. My memory became a nonstop nightmare, as I thought of my parents, my beloved sister, Sarale, and my brothers who had been killed before my eyes. So many times had I whispered to them that we would meet at the Lapusky farm when we escaped Treblinka. Now that I had finally made it here, there was no one left with whom to have a joyous family reunion in freedom. I was alone. I would have to rely on my own guts and wits to survive, to survive and one day tell the world about the atrocities I had seen.

After two weeks Lapusky explained why he could hide me no longer: too many people in the village knew about the Jew hiding in his stable. Both his family's lives and mine would be in great jeopardy if I stayed. Boleslaw's sister Helcha came over that night and cried, wishing that all my family were alive and that they could all have been hidden here. "But we are afraid for your safety now," she said. "And also for our own."

Poles could be executed for harboring Jews, and too many Poles made a business of informing to the Germans. I had no choice. I would have to fend for myself. The Lapuskys gave me some food for the road, but I had nowhere to go.

In Treblinka I had yearned for freedom, but now I saw that freedom also had its perils. I walked in the darkness and cried for all the torture I had endured. "Why, why?" I shouted to no one.

As I went through a field one day I came across some ditches for storing potatoes during the winter. Perhaps, I thought, an empty ditch would be a good place to hide. I dug myself in for a while and tried begging food from farmhouses at night to stave off my hunger. One Saturday night when I emerged to hunt for food I was caught in a drenching rain. Soaked to the bone, I felt myself cursed by G-d. I was hungry and thirsty, mired in dirty mud like a helpless field mouse. I prayed for the Almighty to have mercy on me. I asked why I had been spared, why I had not been killed with the rest of my family. Why would G-d keep me alive for so many months in Treblinka just to torture me now?

Just then I heard someone calling my name. I tried to focus. Who could be calling me so late at night and in such miserable weather? I reached for my only weapon, a small kitchen knife, and wondered if Polish partisans or German soldiers were on my trail. But how would they know my name? Then I thought I recognized the voice.

"Mr. Niewirowsky," I called out, "is that you? Why did you come here? If you wanted to kill me, couldn't you have waited for the rain to stop?"

"Of course not, Saul Kuperhand. I came to protect you from harm, to save you from being killed. I knew you were staying in the potato ditch. Come out and we'll talk."

"Is this a trap Mr. Niewirowsky? I am surprised that someone from such a fine family as yours would be part of a plot to kill me. I knew your parents; they were religious, churchgoing people."

"Please, Kuperhand. I know it is hard for you to trust anyone. Yes, it's crazy to be out in this weather. That's why it was safe to come out and look for you. I have my horse and buggy nearby. I want to take you to my home. Come out and we will talk. Please, I'm getting drenched. Don't be afraid. I come as your friend."

Without any way to confirm that he had come alone, I felt I had no alternative but to trust him. He and his wife had been close friends of my parents. Somehow he must have heard that I was hiding here. I emerged from my hole, and he came over and hugged me.

I apologized for my appearance and smell as we climbed into his buggy. "This jacket must smell bad too. I got it from a corpse in Treblinka the day we planned our escape. I hoped to need the extra warmth when we made good on our plans."

As soon as I arrived at their house Mrs. Niewirowsky burst into tears when she saw how I looked. They covered the windows to make sure no one could see me. As I answered their questions about my parents, family, and Treblinka, Mrs. Niewirowsky sobbed uncontrollably. They brought in plenty of firewood and heated several pots of water. They urged me to throw my clothes into the fireplace and to take a bath. The kindly couple told me not to be ashamed. They were human beings like me, and this was a cruel war. For my own safety and health I must be scrubbed down and my clothes destroyed.

I understood. I must have been a breeding ground for lice, and I had not felt the touch of a scrub brush or of soap since I had left the ghetto a year earlier. Afterward they gave me some straw from the stable to sleep on. Before retiring for the night they fed me some bread, butter, and milk.

Mr. Niewirowsky explained that the *soltis* of the village had let him know that I was hiding in the potato ditch. A major discussion had taken place among the villagers concerning my presence in the area. Some wished to keep it secret that a local Jewish boy was hiding out there, but many others thought the Gestapo would punish them all if I were discovered. Sooner or later the Germans would be informed and would come to kill me. Mr. Niewirowsky heard my name from farmers to whom I had appealed for food, and he felt he could not have my death on his conscience.

I was grateful to G-d that a man with a conscience was to be found in my native country. I slept better that night than at any time in several years, without the usual lice crawling all over me and eating my flesh.

The next morning, a Sunday, Mrs. Niewirowsky woke me at dawn and told me to get dressed. It was Parafialna Niedziela,* a local holiday, and she and her husband were having many people over to their house. It was imperative that I not be around, not even in hiding, because in wartime people could not be trusted. The Niewirowskys gave me breakfast and some food to take with me for the day and told me to hide in the nearby woods until nightfall.

On the way to the forest I was noticed by local shepherds and grooms, older children who cared for the village's sheep and horses. They yelled "Jude," and they pelted me with stones. I walked out of range and sight, afraid that one of these little anti-Semites would report me to the Gestapo. I walked for at least two hours to get safely away from them, only to have a dangerous run-in with a farmer's dog. This vicious dog was not tied up, and in order to escape I had to run toward a man who waved me toward his home.

I was taking a chance by accepting shelter from someone I did not know, but I had no choice. He had a nice smile, and I felt instinctively that I could trust him. The man's name was Anthony Shlewanowsky. He shook my hand, said good morning, and asked with great sincerity and empathy to hear my story.

He crossed himself and even began to sob when the details of Treblinka came to his ears for the first time. He could barely believe that human beings, even Germans, could toss women and children into crematoria like so many logs of firewood. It was hard for him to hear of torture and murder on such a large scale. He saw that not only was I the sole survivor of my family but I was one of the few of an entire generation of Polish Jews to survive.

He grew alarmed when I told him I was seeking the farm of a man whose name I thought was Maximiuk.

"No, no, you don't want to go there," warned Mr. Shlewanowsky. "You have just escaped from hell, and he will only have you sent straight back. Eighteen Jewish men, women, and children hid on his land, paying him much money to conceal them from the German bandits. He took them in, fed them dinner, and built them an underground bunker with special ventilation holes. That first night, when his paying

* Polish for "Parochial (or Parish) Sunday."

guests were asleep, he barred their exit, closed their vents, and suffocated them all. He stripped them of everything they had, including their clothes, and threw their bodies in an old well.

"Believe me," he continued, "you must not go to him. He is certain to kill you as well. You are the only survivor of your family. You must come in and have something to eat. Then you must hide during the daylight hours in the large haystacks in our nearby fields. You will come to me at night until I can connect you with Jewish partisans who come by once in a while. They will know what to do with you and how to keep you alive."

When I accepted the kind man's invitation to enter his house I received a very different reception from his wife and daughters. They became very agitated at the thought that a Jew was in their house. They feared that the Germans would burn down their entire farm for harboring a Jew criminal. His beautiful daughters begged their father to please get me out as soon as I had some bread, butter, and milk.

I was crushed by the discovery that my newfound guardian angel was encumbered by such a fearful and hysterical family. The idea that their father would jeopardize them by extending to me some minimum human compassion brought the girls to tears. What contagious disease did I have that I had to be removed so hurriedly from their home? Surely no one cared about my life, and no one could be trusted.

Realizing this, I did not go straight to the haystacks as planned. I passed them by and picked one out only after much deliberation and observation from a distance. I decided I had better watch the farmer's movements for a time to make sure he could be trusted. I saw him go off to his mill with grain to prepare flour for baking. After it grew dark I saw a wagon pull up to the farmhouse. Would it be Mr. Shlewanowsky returning with some Jewish partisans, as he had promised, or would he be bringing the Gestapo to hunt me down? As nice as Mr. Shlewanowsky seemed, he was under too much pressure for me to trust him with my life.

When only the farmer got out of the wagon I went over and greeted him. He told me that he had not been able to contact the Jewish partisans he knew. The community mill was a center of underground activity, but the Gestapo had been all around the place the whole day. Perhaps the authorities suspected something. He said he felt lucky to have been able to do his business and come home with the flour he needed. With his wife unable to complain about a lack of flour, Mr. Shlewanowsky duly invited me to his home for supper.

The farmer's family seemed calmer about my presence. Perhaps they now trusted me to keep out of sight on their property in broad daylight. I was not able to relax at that meal, however. I kept hearing strange noises outside the kitchen window. Either I was slipping into a dangerous paranoia or there were whispered conversations going on outside the house. Certainly all the activity concerned me, and it was only matter of time before I found out whether I was hearing the farmer's partisan contacts or the Gestapo.

As I watched Mr. Shlewanowsky I was convinced that he was waiting for some sort of signal. Sure enough a whistle could be heard that did not come from an owl, and the farmer went outside to greet a group of men. Expecting the worst, I put my ear to the window to hear their conversation.

Underground Jews

To my great relief the men gathered outside the farmhouse were Jews from Drohiczyn nad Bugium, a town close to Siemiatycze. The farmer was complaining to them about me. He said I did not know how to conduct myself, that I had been walking around during the daytime and was sure to lose my young life. Mr. Shlewanowsky explained to them that I was from Siemiatycze and that I had escaped from Treblinka, where my entire family had been liquidated. He repeated some of my depiction of the death camp to them.

The men said they did not want to meet me. One of them suggested I probably was not a Jew at all but a *Volksdeutscher*. Mr. Shlewanowsky responded with sarcasm and insisted that they meet me. He called for me to come out and introduced me to them.

All their skepticism disappeared when one of them, Carl Carson, recognized me from before the war. He told the others that he knew me from an organization we had both belonged to and that I was a fine person. The group warmed up to me immediately. We exchanged information excitedly, and they were amazed to meet a survivor from Treblinka. They wanted me to dispel the rumors they had heard about the death factory there; instead, I told them that the horrors they had heard about were mild compared to the reality.

These men hid out in various bunkers, and only the younger ones engaged in activities against the Germans. They had only occasional contact with Jewish fighting groups and conducted only limited operations to hamper the German war effort. They had no weapons, and their main objective was survival. They were happy to see someone from Siemiatycze still alive, and they added that they knew of another youth from my town, Hershel Shabbes, who was in contact with the partisans and who provided the underground with medical supplies.

Shabbes was also their reason for fearing the Russian partisans and not coordinating activities with them. On November 15, 1942, he had reported to the partisans about a group of twelve Jews from Siemiatycze he had found in hiding. The Russian partisan leader immediately ordered his men to find out how much gold and currency the Jews had. Shabbes warned the group of refugees about the Jew-hating partisans, and they managed to hide some of their assets under a barn. They could not hide themselves, however, and the partisans killed all twelve of them.

They asked me if I had known about the Siemiatycze survivors, and I said that I had not. All the townsmen I knew had perished in Treblinka, and this additional tragedy was hard to take. Now that I was in Jewish hands, I parted with Mr. Shlewanowsky, thanking him for his kindness. The men told me that they rarely approached this farmhouse so as not to endanger their important contact and his family.

My new companions consisted of three Groody brothers and Carl Carson. They were almost townsmen, but fear seemed to put up a barrier between us. They knew Siemiatycze well since their native town of Drohiczyn nad Bugium was only seven kilometers away. They kept asking me about the procedures in Treblinka, how people were selected, gassed, and turned into ashes. They probably had many relatives and friends who had been put through these procedures. None of them seemed concerned about me, outside of my experiences, until Carl turned their attention to my well-being.

As I stood by observing silently, they discussed what to do with me. Carl wanted to bring me into their hiding place, while the Groody brothers felt this was too dangerous. They argued that it would be better to get me some money so that I could procure my own hiding place with a willing farmer. Carl did not like them treating me as if I were an untrustworthy stranger. He insisted that money could not ensure my safety and that the Groody brothers were trying to buy a solution because they were unwilling to share the risk. They knew very well that without their help I was likely to be found and killed by the Germans.

The Groody brothers insisted that their bunker was too small to share, so Carl offered to share his bunker in the village of Bryki with me. His Polish saviors were a couple named Alexander and Jadwiga Jaggelo. They had hearts of gold and were committed to meeting Carl's basic needs, risking their own lives in the process. They always wore angelic smiles, a trait that they passed on to their lovely daughter, Jashka, and their son, Alexander Jr. They had no objection to my joining Carl in his small bunker beneath their stable. In fact, they extended the bunker so I would have room to lie down after crawling in. Beneath the feeding trough for their horse and cow was a piece of straw-covered wood that concealed the entryway to our bunker. All these precautions meant the difference between life and death should the Gestapo search the premises.

The interior of our bunker also needed special care. The sides were lined with large panels so that they would not cave in and bury us alive. The floor was lined with straw so that we would not be lying on the bare earth. The wooden floor of the stable made up our ceiling. We arranged the floorboards so that the animals' urine would drain to the side, as they stood at the feeding trough, not into our bunker. Some urine did get through, and we had to change our floor straw periodically.

After my experiences on the run, fully exposed to the ravages of nature, I truly appreciated the safety of this bunker. Thanks to the generosity of our hosts, hunger was less a problem than being cramped for space. We greatly looked forward to the safety of the night when we could leave our tiny dungeon and stretch our aching limbs. Breathing fresh air that did not reek of animal urine was also a necessity.

Although Carl took a chance by sharing his bunker with me, I can see how my company kept him sane. We secretly maintained a social life by occasionally visiting a farm family who lived two kilometers away in the village of Norojki. When we met the Zawacka family by accident, we realized we had gained some friends instead of mortal enemies. In fact, we shared a common enemy, since they had a brother, a priest, who had been killed by the Gestapo. When we were able to visit we often shared fine conversation and hearty laughs with the Zawacka sisters, Jadwiga and Zosia, one of whom was married to a shoemaker. This family had a good sense of humor that proved to be valuable therapy in light of the harrowing times we were experiencing.

Our hosts did not have a similar temperament. Mr. Jaggelo worked too hard to socialize in the evening. He was a farm laborer in the employ of the wealthy duke Jan Krakuwka, who was the area's chief landowner. Mr. Jaggelo's domain was a modest one, a small farmhouse and simple barn, and we were the only refugees hidden there. The duke, however, had many barns that he always left open for Jewish fugitives to find temporary shelter in. No destitute or desperate man or woman ever came to the Krakuwka home without being offered food and shelter. The Jewish underground knew that this home was open to them. The duke even won himself the nickname "Avraham Avinu" (Abraham the Patriarch) because of his legendary hospitality.*

Not only did the general populace rarely harbor Jews, but they considered doing so a depraved sin against both G-d and the German authorities. People like Duke Krakuwka who allowed Jewish runaways safe passage endangered both their lives and their estates.

Neighboring Poles hostile to Jews decided to put an end to this philanthropy by informing the Gestapo of Jews hidden on Mr. Jaggelo's property. Fortunately, a sympathetic worker at Gestapo headquarters overheard plans for a raid on Sunday afternoon and tipped off members of the Jewish underground.

The Saturday night before the raid a contingent from the underground came to our barn with the news. The group that delivered the warning included some men from Siemiatycze, among them Hershel Shabbes, Shulke Krawiec, and Irving Morer. If they had not warned us in advance, the Gestapo and their bloodhounds would surely have rooted us out and killed us.

We could not simply flee. First, we had to erase all evidence that our bunker had ever existed. Otherwise the Nazis would have cruelly punished the Jaggelo family. With the help of three of the men who had come to warn us, we removed the wall panels and filled in our bunker with earth. By the time we finished our hard work, not even a human

---

* For Abraham's hospitality see Genesis 18:1–8.

scent was left behind for the bloodhounds to trace. I relocated to Hershel's hideout, while Carl agreed to join a friend and townsman named Pelte in his bunker.

When I arrived at the Shabbes bunker, Hershel's wife, Helen, whose maiden name was Bernstein, tried to calm me down after my tense ordeal. She reminded me that I had been lucky to receive warning in time. Hours later the Gestapo raid took place as scheduled. A unit of Gestapo experts stormed Alexander Jaggelo's farm and demanded to be taken to the hidden Jews. Jaggelo calmly denied harboring any Jews on his property. He told the Germans that even if he were brazenly inclined to break the law he could not have afforded to feed outsiders. He invited the Nazis to see how poor his family was and how they barely had enough food for themselves. Jaggelo also protested that he had no land on which it would be possible to hide anyone. The Gestapo hit him in the face, constantly threatening to harm his family if he did not produce his hidden Jews.

The other members of the Jaggelo family hid with neighbors, but all of them were as good as dead if the Gestapo found proof that the farmer was lying to them. The Germans made a thorough search, but, thankfully, they were unable to turn up any evidence that Jaggelo had been harboring Jews. The angry and frustrated Germans were sure to keep the farmer under surveillance for a while, so Hershel and Helen Shabbes invited me to stay with them for a few weeks.

When their informant in the Gestapo finally gave me the all-clear signal I contacted Mr. Jaggelo and, with his ready permission, began the arduous task of rebuilding the bunker. I thanked the Shabbes family and their network for saving my life and the lives of the righteous Jaggelo family. With many hours of work Carl and I reconstructed our underground shelter with all the original concern for secrecy and more.

It seemed as though I could not go for very long without a major brush with death. After a few weeks in our reconstructed bunker my desire for a decent pair of shoes led me into trouble. My shoes were completely worn and coming apart at the seams. I desperately needed some shoemaker's tools in order to repair them myself, having picked up some shoemaking skills from watching my father at work. One Saturday I told Carl that I would try to reach a shoemaker named Michalek who lived nearby.

It was a moonless night and I became quite disoriented in the extraordinary blackness. I began wandering aimlessly, looking for any light to get my bearings. I finally saw a dim light coming from a stable and I made my way to the door. I called out a friendly greeting to the farmer inside, asking for directions to the shoemaker's house. The man put down his tools and began asking me questions. He wanted to know all about what had happened to my family, how the death camp at Treblinka operated, and even how the crematoria ovens smelled. I was open and frank with him, careful only about not revealing the location of my current hideout.

The man noticed the condition of my shoes and offered to walk me to the shoemaker's house. He stepped inside to tell his wife where he was going and brought out a lantern to light the way in the pitch dark. Somehow we lost each other on the way. Perhaps the lantern went out. I could not tell if I was about to step into a ditch or up a hill. I went back to the farmhouse to wait for my guide. When the farmer's wife saw me return without her husband she became hysterical. She began screaming that I had killed him and refused to listen to my explanation.

The farmers in the area all had metal plates hanging outside their doors to bang on as a signal of trouble. The woman struck this plate with a hammer and soon the noise echoed from one farmhouse to another. When I tried to reason with the woman she simply screamed, cursed, and spat at me. In a matter of minutes I was surrounded by an angry mob of farmers holding lanterns, pitchforks, knives, and axes. They were ready to hack to pieces this stranger accused of a heinous crime by a screaming housewife.

Fortunately some of the older, wiser men stepped forward and said there was no reason to act rashly. I was unarmed and I was not going anywhere. There was neither blood on my hands nor any other evidence of wrongdoing. The mob decided to wait a while and investigate when, finally, the farmer appeared, alive and well. He explained the whole situation to the crowd and put them all at ease. He himself could not say how he had gotten lost so close to home when his lantern failed. He found himself going in circles until he finally made it home in time to save my life from instant "justice."

The farmer recovered enough from his ordeal to want to escort me to Michalek's place. He not only took me to the shoemaker's door but told me how much I deserved to have my shoes worked on. He repeated to Michalek many of the details of my Treblinka experience, telling him that I was a local boy whose family had been reduced to ashes and smoke. The craftsman quickly cobbled my dilapidated footwear into something resembling real shoes. After such a harrowing experience I would have been grateful just to return to my bunker alive.

Despite the danger Carl and I did not stop our excursions to the outside world. Saturday night was the safest, quietest night for us to walk around. The farmers were usually resting at home and the Germans were busy getting drunk before their Sunday off. Carl was especially eager to risk the roads after an uncle told him that his young stepbrother was still alive.

The boy's story was tragic even in a time of great tragedies. He had been hiding out in dense shrubbery with four siblings and his mother, who had raised Carl after his own mother had died giving birth to him. As inevitably happened to those without the active protection of local Poles, the hidden family was soon spotted and reported to the Gestapo. A heavily armed German unit came running, as if a Jewish family in hiding posed a serious threat to the mighty Third Reich. The Germans followed the Polish informer to the Jews' hideout and soon rooted out the woman and her children.

The hysterical mother begged for mercy, amusing the Nazis by crawling on her knees and kissing their hands. When she realized that the Germans were going to mow down the entire family with their automatic weapons, she pleaded with the soldiers to allow her to cover her children with a blanket so they would not see the rifles pointed at them. This kind indulgence the Nazis allowed. They also gave the Polish informer the privilege of finishing off the family, permitting him to strip the bodies of their clothing and to search for any hidden valuables.

One of the children, a ten-year-old boy, had managed to escape the massacre. He had been away from the hideout and spotted the Germans coming for his family. His instincts told him to run in the opposite direction. Had he paused to warn his family he would have been killed along with them. He had not had a chance to say good-bye, but at least he had been spared the trauma of seeing them shot.

The boy remembered that his father had told him about a friendly farmer they could go to in an emergency. He followed the directions his father had given and sure enough found the farm. The farmer recognized the boy immediately and took him in as a shepherd. Many such orphaned children worked on farms. The boy had blond hair and blue eyes and spoke Polish perfectly. It entailed no great risk, therefore, to give shelter to this typically Polish-looking boy. The farmer gave him the Polish name Stashek and allowed him to live and work on the farm for the duration of the war.

When Carl discovered Stashek's whereabouts, I went with him to see his stepbrother. In an emotional reunion the two hugged and kissed, clinging to the remnants of their family. It was painful for Carl to hear of the deaths of his loving stepmother and her other children. It was miraculous that Stashek had survived the slaughter and was ensconced at a Polish farm. Carl judged that Stashek was probably safer where he was, living the life of a Polish shepherd boy, than hiding out as a Jew in our bunker. We parted company and promised to make the long trip to visit as often as we safely could.

Eventually the decision to leave Stashek on his own began to bother Carl. Although his position seemed secure, something could happen to expose the boy's background. What would prevent a neighbor from reporting his suspicions to the Germans? Carl needed to talk the matter over with family and there was only one other family member with whom he could consult. Carl and I left our bunker on the following Saturday night to visit his uncle, Hershel Resnick. The Resnicks, who were also from the town of Drohiczyn nad Bugium, were hiding nearby.

As we crossed an open field on the way to the Resnicks we noticed the shadow of a person who seemed to be following us. I told Carl to ready his gun because we had no cover in the field and the person coming toward us might be a Polish bandit or a German soldier. When the man was close enough to be caught in Carl's flashlight I told Carl to put his gun down. I instinctively recognized the man as a fellow Jew. He turned out to be a Jewish tailor from the town of Czyżew. His name was Shloime, and he wept to find us. He told us that he had been forced to leave his hiding place and begged us to let him stay with us for a couple of days. Although we were already very cramped, we agreed to take him in temporarily and to see what we could do for him.

The three of us had walked for about an hour when we suddenly seemed to be surrounded by German soldiers on horseback combing the area with flashlights. This was obviously a search party investigating a report of nighttime activity. Perhaps we had been spotted, or perhaps they were on the trail of partisans. In any case they would surely shoot us on sight. Without any buildings nearby our only hope was to crawl to the row of hedges that dissected the field we were traversing. Luckily our clothes were black, and we reached the short but thick bushes before the sweeping flashlights caught us. To avoid capture and certain death we had to enmesh ourselves completely among the hedges, not exposing any part of our bodies to the systematic search of the German soldiers.

Crawling into the prickly hedges was painful. The thorns and bristles cut into us, and we had to get off the ground where there was only the narrow trunk of the bush. Shloime was having trouble forcing himself deeper into the hedge where his feet would not be seen. He complained that he could not do it, and we had to push him and even threaten to strike him with the butt of our rifle. As I struggled to tuck myself completely into a bush a sharp pain shot through my hand. I had cut myself on a piece of glass and was bleeding badly. I suppressed a scream and tried to stop the bleeding.

The mounted soldiers moved past us and slowly made their way down the field. I would have a scar on my hand for the rest of my life, but we were most fortunate to walk away from this dangerous situation. If the Nazis had brought along a dog we would have been finished.

We had lost too much time hiding and would not be able to get back to our bunker before daybreak. This meant that we would have to find a new hiding place for the day. We made our way back to a barn near a farmhouse that we had passed. We would have to risk hiding in the hayloft until nightfall. We began to lose patience with Shloime, who was the wrong person to be with in such a difficult situation. After we had hidden ourselves in the hayloft, he asked me what we were going to eat. Incredulous at the question, I said, "Why nothing, of course." He even asked me if it was all right to smoke. We were amazed that he had not yet learned any of the hard lessons about survival in this war.

We tried to make Shloime understand the need for extra caution when people came into the barn, but sure enough he sneezed when the farmer was there early that morning.

"Who is there?" the farmer asked.

Given no choice, Carl and I came down from the hayloft and confronted the farmer. We let him see our rifle but decided to address him politely: "Please forgive us for this intrusion. We are not bandits or killers and have no intention of harming you, your family, or your possessions. We were passing through last night and were forced to take shelter here by a German search party. We will wait here until dark. We don't want anyone to get hurt. If you try to contact the German authorities we will have no choice but to turn your farm into a battlefield. You can see our rifle. We have more grenades and ammunition in the loft. Hitler has made us into desperate people, so don't try to get in our way."

Just then the farmer's wife called him in to breakfast. Carl ran to cover the barn door and urged the farmer not to go back to his house unless he could so so without raising his wife's suspicions. By that time, however, the wife had responded to her husband's delay by coming to the barn. Now we faced a stickier situation. As she entered, the sight of her husband and the armed strangers frightened her. I quickly went to calm her down so she would not scream and alert any others.

"Please don't be afraid of us," I implored. "We are not bandits, G-d forbid. We are decent human beings like you are. Circumstances have brought us here and we will leave your barn at nightfall. Now that you have seen us, however, we can't let you leave. You will come to no harm, and we are just doing what we must to stay alive in this cruel war."

The woman began to cry. "But my baby is in the house resting in a crib. I must go in to my baby."

"Of course you should go to your baby. But we can't have people coming to your house and asking where your husband is. You might reveal to them that he is being kept in the barn by partisans. It is too risky to let you stay in the house now. We know the Germans are close, and there will be a big fight if they are brought here. Your husband is sure to be killed by the Nazis, and they won't hesitate to kill your child as well. If you do nothing to compromise our presence then I can assure you that no one will get hurt."

She crossed herself and swore to G-d not to reveal any knowledge of us. "I will bring my husband's breakfast here to him and then get breakfast for all of you," she said. "If anyone comes to the house I will tell them that I am not feeling well, that I have a fever. No one will bother us."

True to her word she did not try to alert the authorities. She not only brought us breakfast but also supper at the end of the day. We kept the farmer with us all day and remained on good terms. We apologized again for the inconvenience we had caused and thanked them for their kindness under the circumstances. By the time we left them at night-fall we were almost friends.

Carl and I had had enough of Shloime's company, so we parted ways. We took back our invitation to join us temporarily in our bunker. I wondered if Shloime would be able to survive the war on his own. I got the answer years later at a gathering in New York. When I met Shloime I reminded him of our experience hiding in the bushes from the Germans. I asked him if he thought we would have survived if I had not been so brutal with him at the time. I showed him the scar on my hand, my constant souvenir of that close encounter with death.

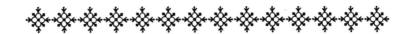

When Skeletons Throw Their Weight Around

The close calls of our recent forays scared us into staying near our bunker for some time afterward. Given the urine-soaked earth that surrounded our enclosure, we could only stand being inside for limited periods of time. We needed to get out to stretch our legs and breathe some fresh air. Still, we greatly appreciated the safety of our bunker beneath the cattle trough, and we thanked G-d every time we returned to it alive. Despite the danger we also continued to visit the Zawacka family. As young people we needed the change of atmosphere to momentarily forget the insanity of war.

We were on our way to the Zawackas one night when we heard someone walking in our direction. We readied our rifle and flashlight. One had to be on the lookout for Polish bandits and Jew-hunters, who killed Jews and stripped them to the bone looking for hidden valuables. When we challenged the stranger he identified himself as Izac Helfinger from the city of Kielce. He and another man had escaped from Treblinka II during a revolt. Most of the escapees had been killed, but he was one of the lucky few to make it this far.

I told him about my own escape shortly after the revolt in which he had taken part. We recounted in detail the events of that sunny afternoon when a woman who had attempted to escape had been hung upside down from a pole. He knew enough of the details to convince me that he was telling the truth about being at Treblinka. He then told us how he had survived in the meantime and how he had become separated from his companion.

He and his friend had found shelter with a poor farmer who could barely feed his wife and grown daughter. After two weeks the farmer told them to look for shelter elsewhere, but Izac's friend made the farmer a proposal. As a skilled tanner he could bring them a handsome income making saddles and other leather accessories. He did not look or sound Jewish and was willing to marry their daughter and live as their Polish son-in-law. Between his masterful work on hides and their daughter's attraction to him, he convinced them that he would be a valuable asset to their family farm.

"An obvious Jew like myself was not about to be the best man at their Polish wedding," Izac said with some bitterness. "Their nuptial agreement stipulated that I was a liability that had to get going. Going where? I don't know. I don't know anyone around here. I am wandering like Cain, without food or money. Most importantly, I have no shelter. I could be killed at any moment. I am so desperate that I too would think about marrying a farmer's very ugly daughter."

Izac moved us with his desperate situation as well as his humor. We understood how his friend could marry a sow in times like this. It was hard not to empathize with a fellow escapee from Treblinka. I pulled Carl aside for a private conversation, suggesting that we take Izac into our bunker. But Carl reminded me of how precarious our own situation already was. We had a tiny shelter with no room for a third person, and we already had trouble paying our hosts for our small share of food.

I appealed to Carl with the weight of Jewish law: "We cannot leave a person in such a dangerous situation. You know that Izac will not live out the week in his current state. If G-d continues to help us survive, he will do so by the merit of this act of sacrifice. Do we want Izac's death on our conscience for the rest of our lives? Surely we would deserve punishment for leaving him out here to wander until he is shot or starves to death."

We talked it over for an hour before Carl finally relented. The Jaggelos would have to give their permission first. We approached our Polish hosts and saviors and asked them to allow one more soul to survive
in our bunker beneath their barn. Every scrap of news we heard gave
us hope that the Germans would soon retreat to their old borders. We
assured the Jaggelos that the war would soon end and the terrible danger it posed to us all would finally cease. So angelic were they that they
agreed to take on this additional risk. No words can express our gratitude to this family for their integrity and generosity in the difficult years
of 1943 and 1944.

Meanwhile, the most horrendous news continued to reach us. Jews
were constantly being murdered. The Germans exterminated whole
communities made up of thousands of people, while Polish bandits
hunted down small groups of refugees. We heard about one Jewish
mother and daughter who lived miserably in an underground bunker
under a stable. Unlike us, however, they did not have the consent of
the farmer to live there. Many Jews who tried to protect their burrows
from the elements could not get permission from the owner of the
house or barn under which they hid.

This particular mother would crawl out of her hole at night to forage for food. Sadly, she was caught and killed by Polish bandits. Without her mother to feed her, the child perished soon afterward.

These painful reports of Polish bandits preying on helpless Jews
enraged our friend Hershel Shabbes. The idea that local civilians furthered the Nazi holocaust made his nights sleepless ones. These Poles
would hunt down the Jewish refugees who emerged at night to look for
food. While some of them were bounty hunters rewarded by the Gestapo, others killed Jews for the sport. Hershel discussed with us how
we might organize to defend Jewish refugees against the barbarism of
these bloodthirsty pirates.

Hershel gathered a number of Jews together and they pooled their
resources. To carry out their plan they would need some Polish and
Russian army uniforms, currency from various countries, communications equipment, and plenty of guns and ammunition. They soon acquired four guns, including two automatic rifles that could fire up to
seventy-two rounds of ammunition. They did not have the manpower
to confront the local killers directly, but they intended to throw their

weight around with enough authority to intimidate the people of the region. Their main weapons would have to be psychological, because they had no support from the local citizens or Polish partisans. All Germans and Poles, with a few glorious exceptions, were the enemy. Jews could not even depend on Gentile doctors for medical supplies or attention.

Our partisans had little more than Hershel's leadership and their own desperation. They all faced death daily anyway, so they had no need to summon extra bravery or daring. Having assembled the required uniforms, weapons, and paraphernalia, they planned a major operation to put the fear of a Jewish underground into the craven hearts of the local bandits. One Saturday night they marched into the village of Lopusze and pounded on the door of the mayor, the old *soltis* of the village. As he and some onlookers gaped at their uniforms and guns, the partisans asked "permission" to link their telephone equipment to his phone line. "It is extremely urgent," they assured him. "We must get an important call through to our liaison headquarters in Moscow."

They looked very official as they ran yards of wire through the mayor's window and "connected" the field telephone to his phone line. They then unrolled a large military map and began to bark out positions of troop movements. Dressed in a Russian officer's uniform, one of the men, who spoke Russian perfectly, burst in to report that the village of Lopusze was fully secured and completely surrounded. This they repeated over their bogus telephone link to Moscow. They loudly reviewed an inventory of military supplies received by parachute drop, detailing the guns and ammunition that they had distributed to partisan units at various locations.

One partisan even spoke broken English, putting through a call to military headquarters in London. None of the Polish farmers could tell that this was a bluff or that the communications hookup went nowhere. To add authenticity, the ersatz general, Hershel Shabbes, asked the mayor for a supply of vodka to maintain the morale of his men and to keep them warm at night. The high-ranking pretender offered to pay, making an impressive display of Russian rubles, German marks, English pounds, American dollars, and Polish zlotys to convince the mayor that these partisans had international support. It did not matter that only one bottle of vodka was procured.

"General" Shabbes then ordered that twenty farmers report immediately, each bringing his own wagon. He told the mayor that the partisans needed the wagons to deliver large quantities of ammunition to
various units in the area. Hershel assured the mayor, in a typically military tone that wavered between generosity and intimidation, that all
the villagers would be compensated for participating in this military
convoy. The smooth execution of orders would prevent any unneces-
sary commandeering of civilian equipment. Each farmer was to come
with a large cotton sack and a length of cord. Every stop on their nighttime supply run was planned so the wagons and drivers could return
to their farms by sunrise. The mayor soon had a dozen men running
to nearby farms to retrieve the required vehicles and drivers for this
major military operation against the Germans.

As word of the powerful Jewish partisan army spread like wildfire
the twenty wagons arrived on time at the mayor's home. The farmers
were made to wear the large sacks over their heads so that they would
not be able to identify the underground operatives riding with them
as they went about dropping off ammunition at pre-planned locations.
The "ammunition" consisted of loosely packed cases of rocks and metal debris that made a ruckus as they bounced on the buckboards. The
operation woke up almost everyone along the route as the wagons
stopped to make their phantom deliveries.

At various farmhouses the Polish men under the sacks filled excited farmers in on the breaking news and urged them to donate some
food to the partisans and to promise not to inform the Germans. The
Jewish underground got some much-needed food out of the operation
as well as the fear and respect of every Pole in the region. If one of the
Poles tried to free himself from his sack, his escort nudged him with a
gun barrel—or, in most cases, something that felt like one. The partisans spoke loudly to their nonexistent contacts in the woods, calling out
many names and convincing the unseeing Polish wagon owners that
dozens of partisan units were receiving these deliveries of ammunition.

The sun would soon rise, so the ruse had to end. Each partisan got
off his wagon under cover of some woods and sent the horses galloping down the road. It took the farmers a while to realize they were alone
and to remove the sacks that had kept them from seeing how few men
the Jewish underground really had. By the time the Poles worked them-

selves free the partisans had disappeared. As successful as Gideon's military subterfuge in the Bible,* the action of the large and well-connected Jewish partisan army became the talk of the region. That Sunday the mayor and the captive Lopusze wagoners were nothing less than celebrities in every local church, eagerly sought out for details about the heavily armed and well-organized force operating in the woods.

We aimed primarily to stop the murderous activity of the Polish bounty hunters, and we achieved this objective. It seemed much too dangerous to provoke the Jews now that armed partisans were everywhere and the German hold on the region was doomed. We knew that the Gestapo would step into the charged atmosphere, but we had little to lose.

The inevitable Polish informers contacted the Germans and soon the Gestapo placed the poor mayor and his villagers under interrogation. The Poles stammered that they had been forced by armed men to cooperate. They had not given any information about the location of German headquarters. Now they did their best to recall details that would be of use to the Nazi authorities. Those details only threw the poor Germans into a tizzy of confusion and fear.

What did the Poles mean when they said they heard conversations in Russian, French, and English, as well as in Polish? How had these men acquired currency from these countries? What sort of communications equipment did they have? How large was the map they were reading? What kinds of ammunition were dropped and who had seen evidence of parachute material? How much ammunition was delivered and to what locations? About how many partisans were involved and which armies were supplying them?

The Germans' bullying and threatening manner of questioning only encouraged the farmers to exaggerate further the partisan threat they had faced before giving up their wagons and food supplies. The Germans beat the mayor bloody and repeatedly demanded to know why they had not been informed about the incident more quickly. Members of the Nazi network of informants began to accuse each other of dual loyalty. This most distasteful element of the local populace shuddered in fear. The local Gestapo had good cause to suspect that its intelligence

* For Gideon's military exploits see Judges 7–8.

system was full of holes. It seemed likely that higher-ups were underestimating the danger to German control in the region. The local men knew that the reality of the Russian front was likely to be even worse than the bad news they were receiving.

We prepared not only to defend against a huge German response but to take advantage of it. We intentionally left many tracks for the Gestapo to follow leading to the homes of the leaders of armed Polish gangs that terrorized Jewish refugees. Unlike the Jews, these thugs did not hide in underground bunkers when the Gestapo came after them with automatic weapons. In the ensuing gun battles the Nazis wiped out many of these killers. Moreover, as the German forces followed the retreating armed Poles into the forests, they took many casualties themselves. A plague on both their houses! We laid low while our two bitterest foes destroyed each other.

A poignant personal matter became mixed up in the ensuing battles. Duke Krakuwka from the village of Bryki, whose barns and lands harbored many hidden Jewish refugees, had a son who helped the Polish nationalist partisans, the Armia Krajowa.* Young Bolek often met with the AK in its hideouts in the Brzezinski forest, telling these killers where they could find helpless Jews to plunder and murder. Instead of coordinating activities with Jewish partisans in the woods, they would attack Jewish groups at every opportunity.

A group of hidden Jews sent a delegate, Shloime Groody, to tell the old duke about his son's activities. When Bolek continued to instigate attacks against Jews, a group of partisans from Siemiatycze and Drohiczyn nad Bugium warned the duke that his son would be shot if he failed to stop helping the AK murder Jews. It was an unpleasant task to confront him this way, since this righteous Gentile was the savior of many Jews. Obliged to deliver a large quota of his dairy and farm goods to the county seat in Narik, the man known as "Avraham Avinu" consistently undersupplied the Germans because of all the milk, cheese, eggs, and butter that he gave instead to Jewish refugees hiding on his lands.

One day the mayor of Bryki took the duke to task for falling short of his quota. The Polish *soltis* accused him of allowing his cows to be milked by Jews so that the Germans got far less than they demanded. The may-

* See the note on p. 76.

or was about to report the duke to the Nazi authorities, which meant that the landowner and his family would be executed, his farm destroyed, and all his lands scoured for hidden Jews. The Jewish partisans had to step in quickly; many Jewish lives were at stake. The leading partisans, Hershel Shabbes and Peisach Cimbalist, paid a visit to the mayor of Bryki.

The Saturday night before the duke was to be exposed, several armed partisans entered the mayor's home at a time when they would not be observed. They confronted him about spreading word among the villagers that the duke was not providing his quota of goods to the Germans, striking him in the face and body. Since this treacherous coward was so eager to meet the Germans' quota, they gave him more to worry about than just the duke's undersized contributions. They brought the mayor over to the piles of dairy goods ready to be brought to Nazi headquarters and spilled out many gallons of milk. Then they smashed many dozens of eggs that were stacked up ready for delivery to the occupying power.

"If you report to the Nazis about the Jews being hidden and fed at the Krakuwka estate," they declared, "you will all be included in the Germans' retaliation. They will execute many farmers and burn down most of your homes. If any of you survive the Nazis, we Jewish partisans will come and finish you off." They continued, "Now all of you have a quota problem, not just the duke. It is time you cowards learned a lesson in resistance. Maybe we'll teach you how to be a patriotic Pole defending his land against foreign invaders. You may tell the other farmers about what we have done here tonight, but I doubt you'll tell the Nazis."

The partisans took as much butter as they could carry, leaving the bruised mayor of Bryki to deal with his new supply problem. Ironically, the only dairy supplies that were not destroyed came late, and undersized as usual, from the Krakuwka estate. The duke himself came to the mayor's home that Sunday morning and saw the damage. The mayor sobbed and embraced the man he had been ready to turn in to the Nazis. "I don't need your milk and eggs now, Mr. Krakuwka. Look at what the Jewish partisans did to me and my delivery pile." The good-hearted duke sympathized with the mayor's situation.

Aware by now of the increased partisan activity, the Nazis realized that they would have to loot the local farms on an individual basis rather than collectively. Instead of resenting the Jews, the farmers had gained a new respect for them. The Jewish partisans had won back a bit of dignity with their daring acts of resistance. No longer did Jews in our area fear being murdered or reported to the Gestapo. For the rest of the war we were able to concentrate on one enemy only, the Germans.

Slowly but surely the front lines approached our region. Our angelic hosts, the Jaggelos, were able to assume the added risk of harboring Izac Helfinger because the beginning of the end was finally in sight. At night, as we hid in our underground bunker, we could hear the artillery blasts coming closer with each passing day. We prayed to G-d that we would survive the terrible wave of destruction that had washed over the continent for the past several years.

One night an excited Mr. Jaggelo came to our bunker with some news. A division of Russian partisans had arrived, led by an officer named Colpac. They had parachuted into the forests near the front lines and were recruiting volunteers from among the escapees from German prisoner-of-war camps. Equipped by Russian parachute drops, these guerrillas plagued the German army with hit-and-run strikes and missions of sabotage. Knowing the German prison camps all too well, these hardened partisans of Colpac's *Otriad* (unit) successfully attacked several camps and freed the inmates.

As their numbers swelled, the powerful partisans operated more openly, daring to strike against the Nazi railroads and communications systems in broad daylight. They were effectively preparing the area for the advance of the regular Soviet army. We were tempted to join this growing partisan army, but we Jews had reservations about doing so. Many of the partisans were Ukrainians who had served as volunteer guards in the death camps and forced labor camps. Sadistic Jew-haters and murderers, they could not be trusted as comrades in arms.

To save themselves from being killed by the advancing Russians or the retreating Germans, these rats ran into the forests when the partisans attacked their camps. They were smart enough to know that the Gestapo they adored would butcher them to prevent them from testifying about the atrocities they themselves had delighted in. When these volunteer camp guards made it to the forests they simply lied to the partisans about their roles in the camps. They claimed that they were prisoners, victims instead of victimizers.

Despite this rotten element in the partisan ranks Carl was excited about taking his gun and striking a blow against the Germans as a member of Colpac's partisans. Carl was a big-hearted fellow but too impulsive for his own good.

"Not so fast, Carl," I told him. "I think you would be making the biggest mistake of your life. You have other reasons to live, other people to live for. Don't forget your responsibilities to your surviving stepbrother, Stashek, who is living on a nearby farm as a shepherd. You are the only father that boy has. You have more to live for than I do. My whole family is ashes at Treblinka. I want to survive for their memory, but you can be the difference in Stashek's life. Do you know what I'd give to see my beloved little sister, Sarale, to be able to give her a future?

"We must fight just to survive. We owe it to our families, our generation, our people. Who would you be fighting for? Half the men in the partisan unit would want to see you dead. If you are wounded, they will surely leave you to rot. They won't hesitate to kill a Jew when the opportunity arises. You may not even get a chance to fight any Germans with them."

Our argument became so heated that we forgot ourselves and began to shout. Carl tried to win the debate by pointing the rifle at my head and threatening to shoot. Mrs. Jaggelo had to come to our bunker and reprimanded Carl for screaming so loud that he could be heard by neighbors walking by.

"We could be reported to the Germans and have our family killed and our farm burned to the ground," she told us. "Now what is going on between you two that could make you forget yourselves this way?"

We affectionately called Mrs. Jaggelo "Mom" and told her what our argument was about. Unlike her husband, Mrs. Jaggelo sided with me in the controversy. Joining Colpac's partisans would be suicide.

"Carl, you are very stubborn," she began. "You'd better listen to your friend Saul. He thinks before he acts, while you have too hot a temper. How do you think Saul managed to get away from Treblinka and survive this long? You'd better listen to him and to me. I suffer plenty for the three of you. It is not easy having sleepless nights worrying about our safety here. I always pray for G-d to help us make it through this war without being killed.

"Now that we are so close to the end you want to get yourself killed?

Maybe I should be glad to be rid of you. I would certainly sleep better with you gone. No. Listen to your friend Saul and stay in your hiding place for a while longer."

Carl quieted down. The only noise was the convincing argument made by the approaching artillery bombardments. The retreating German army came very close to us when it appropriated an empty house on the nearby Krakuwka farm as a kitchen and mess hall. With German soldiers digging in at the farm, we knew our bunker was no longer safe. If the Germans did not find us themselves the artillery shells might. The wooden barn above us would certainly go up in flames if it were hit, and we would be buried alive in the rubble. We had to build a new shelter in an open field, where soldiers would not go. The Jaggelos would begin the task in the daylight, telling their neighbors that they were digging a bomb shelter, and we would do most of the work at night.

To prepare for the worst we made two separate tunnels to the bunker. We decorated the inside with Christian symbols to make people think that this bomb shelter harbored local Poles. We dug zigzagged entrance and exit tunnels so that grenades thrown in by the Nazis would not reach us inside. We worked feverishly to stay ahead of the German troops, stocking the bunker with enough food and water to sustain us for weeks.

When I first learned that the Nazis were moving into the empty house on the Krakuwka estate I knew we had another problem besides the possibility of being discovered by them. I had stored our extra ammunition in that house's abandoned chimney. When the Germans installed an army stove and hooked it up to that chimney the ammunition would explode. After losing a few army cooks, the angry Germans would be certain to take revenge on the duke and his family.

Carl yelled at me for storing our ammunition in the chimney. "So you are the smart one, are you? Now the Krakuwkas will be killed, we will all be killed, because the Germans will know that this area is a center of partisan activity. How could you do a thing like this?"

I could only respond that I had not known that the empty house would one day be used by the Germans. But I had caused the problem, so now I had to fix it.

The presence of German soldiers all over the farm made my mission quite dangerous. I put on Mr. Jaggelo's big farm coat to conceal

the rifle strapped on my shoulder and went outside with a pail of potatoes. I began calling "*Malush! Malush!*" (the usual Polish feeding call)
to the free-roaming pigs. The chore of feeding the pigs took me past
the Germans and all the way to the chimney. It looked as if the Germans had finished setting up their army mess hall, so I probably reached
the chimney in the nick of time. It could well have blown up that very
night. I reached up and pulled out the bullets and grenades I had stored
there, placing them beneath the last potatoes in my large pail. The
Germans never suspected that the pig farmer walking among them was
a Jew carrying ammunition.

I buried the ordnance in a nearby valley, carefully concealing any
trace of my digging. When I arrived back at our bunker I took a deep
breath of relief. Strolling around out in the open seemed too great a
risk to take, especially with our anticipated day of deliverance so close.
Only my moral responsibility to the good duke had made me risk so
much at this time.

Our new bunker was literally under the Germans' noses, but we were
quite far below ground. With German jackboots treading above our
heads we prayed to G-d for several more weeks of His miraculous protection. Not all of us had had the nerve to stay here when the German
retreat flooded the area with troops. When Izac Helfinger saw the
Germans coming he fled our shelter so fast that he left one of his shoes
behind. He headed for the Zawacka farm as if he knew that the Germans would discover our bunker—which they eventually did.

They shouted down to us, "Who is there? Identify yourselves."

I considered not answering, but that might bring a grenade in our
faces. I decided to respond in Polish and hoped that the soldiers would
not order us to emerge. I told them we were Poles who had run away
from the village of Rogawka, a town that I had heard had just been liberated by Russian troops.

Apparently my answer was the right one. The Germans figured that
anyone who ran away from the Soviets must be on their side. Nonetheless, they sent a soldier down through one of our tunnels to investigate.
I could not believe that I, a hunted Jew, was conversing with a German
soldier. I spoke in my best Polish and made a point of pretending not
to understand German when he asked me if I had any weapons or
ammunition.

"*Waffen?* Oh, we are here to run away from the weapons."

The soldier searched our bunker with his flashlight, seeing all the Christian artifacts that we had positioned for just such an inspection. A second German soldier crawled in to see how the search was going. If they had done some serious poking with their rifles they would have found enough evidence to earn us our eternal rest in this self-dug grave.

"Nothing suspicious to report here. These are just some Poles hiding out from the Russian advance," said the soldier who much preferred to be somewhere else.

They crawled out without so much as a good-bye. They were the last German soldiers I would ever see.

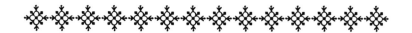

Liberated, Not Free

*I*t was September 1944. It took only a few short days for the thunderous shells to roll past us. The soldiers we now saw wore the uniform of the Red Army. The war was over for us. We were no longer marked for instant death.

A flood of emotions rose from somewhere deep inside. I sobbed uncontrollably for untold hours. Was I dreaming? Was the day of liberation truly at hand? Was I free? Could I leave the subterranean world of moles and worms? Could I walk the streets in broad daylight like a human being? Could I speak aloud?

I could not stop feeling, but I did not know if I should feel joy or sorrow. I had made it through. I had survived against impossible odds. But where was my entire generation, my entire family, my parents, my brothers, and my dear little sister, Sarale? What could I do, how could I live without them? What was my life worth without them?

I tried to settle myself down, to return to the world of the living. I went to see the Zawacka family, who had been such an important island of normalcy in our years of hell. I had promised them that if I survived the war I would build them an oven that would warm their entire house. I also built them a combination stove and oven for cooking and baking. At that time these were luxury items for farmers in Poland. It comforted me greatly to throw myself into my old work and to thank them in this way for all their kindness.

Before I made my way back to my native town of Siemiatycze I also had to thank the entire Jaggelo family, including Mr. and Mrs. Alexander Jaggelo, their son, Alexander Jr., and their daughter, Jadwiga. There are no words to express my gratitude for their goodness, their sacrifice. They assumed great risks by allowing Carl and me to hide beneath their barn. We said good-bye with tears in our eyes, since they were like a second family to both of us. Who knows whether we would have survived without them? We would never forget what they had done for us.

Carl and I also went to bid farewell to the noble, kind, and generous Duke Krakuwka and his wife. Who knows how many Jews this courageous couple saved from annihilation? Surely the Lord has granted them eternal life in the world of the righteous.

I left this place of living death and took the road to my birthplace. On the way to Siemiatycze I sat down on a large rock and wept.

"Rock, you are so much better off than I am. You have no heart full of pain. You are solid; you have your place here. You are not looking for anyone or anything. But I, I have no place. Not here, not anywhere. Where are my roots now? Where is my home and family? Where do I eat or sleep now?"

I turned to my Rock in Heaven and continued to cry, wetting the old piece of bread I had unwrapped from my small bundle of possessions, my life savings.

When I arrived in Siemiatycze the population consisted mostly of ghosts, together with a few miraculous survivors. Most uplifting to me was the sight of an intact Jewish family. This family, which I quickly attached myself to, was headed by a furrier named Shloime Grodzicki and his wife, Roiske. Their children were Moishe, a young fellow my age with whom I had been friendly before the war, a young girl, Rochele, and a teenaged girl, Miriam, who was a bit younger than me.

I was not the only rolling stone that came to their house in search of a home. The abandoned house that they moved into became the center of communal life for the town's Jewish survivors, and we all became unnaturally close in the emotionally charged and still dangerous atmosphere in which we lived. While our part of Poland had been liberated, the war would rage on for another three months.

The furrier's house was a truly Jewish home, always open to the needy. At such a hungry time selfishness was natural, yet he gave with open hands to the destitute survivors who straggled in. I know because I was one of them. No sooner had I arrived than he invited me to wash up and prepare for lunch.

"My house is your house," he said warmly, preparing a place for me to stay. He knew I was full of pain and let me talk at my own pace. "Don't be shy," he told me. "Tell us anything you want to say."

Miriam came over to me as I finished my meal. I remembered seeing her years ago. My friend's sister had been a beautiful young girl, always full of life. I could picture her smiling, laughing, being polite, and making others feel comfortable. Now she was older and much more serious. The war had reshaped her beauty but had not diminished it. But I was not prepared for the verbal assault with which she greeted me.

"Saul Kuperhand, did you remove our family's possessions from their hiding place? You are the only other person who knew about it. You helped us hide our valuables in a buried barrel and built an oven over it in our little storage cellar. While we were still hiding in our ghetto bunker we found out that our barrel was missing. We sent Moishe out one night when we had run out of food. There wasn't a scrap to be found, so he decided to dig out our barrel and buy some contraband food. When Moishe got inside our house all the furniture was missing. When he reached the storage cellar he saw that the entire oven and the barrel buried beneath it were gone. We couldn't imagine how anyone else could have known about it or discovered it."

She was not accusing me directly, but I felt wounded by the implication.

"It is all right if you dug it out to pay some Poles for food or protection. We understand completely if you did."

Speechless, I put my head in my hands from pain and embarrassment. I had not done any such thing. How could she even ask?

Miriam immediately realized her mistake. She apologized profusely for asking silly questions. We got off to a terrible start, but it was impossible to ignore her. By the time Miriam was convinced that I had forgiven her, even her father knew that there was something developing between us.

I remembered Shloime as an excellent furrier in the prewar days when I would visit Moishe. Now, without any currency to be earned or spent, it was imperative to find work that could be bartered for food. Shloime had many more opportunities to turn sheepskins into coats than I had to build ovens, so I joined the men of my extended family who plunged into the furrier trade to stave off starvation. In exchange for our work the farmers would not only give us more skins to work on but also basic foods.

I saw a lot of Miriam in that kitchen and recalled that she had caught my eye years earlier, before the war. Whenever I finished my work in the fur factory and she could take a break from her cooking and cleaning we talked about our past experiences. She learned about the horrors I had seen in Treblinka and I heard about her years of living underground. It seems as though we had both been reborn, because both of us had been buried alive for years. The first time I held her hand I realized that I was truly alive, that Miriam was alive, and that new life could bloom in the glow of our embrace. Even before I realized that we were falling in love, other people seemed to give us encouraging glances, as if to say, "Yes! Make a future for yourselves. Prove to us that the world will learn to laugh and live again."

We soon felt that we were *bashert* (destined) for each other. I began to feel that G-d had kept me alive to marry this wonderful girl. From that time on I could not imagine life without her. Whenever I thought about my survival and the idea that I might soon be married, an eerie memory kept reappearing: I was back in the ghetto with my family. We were in that long line waiting to be transported to Treblinka. The president of the *Judenrat* was saying, "What is your rush? You are not going to a wedding."

I had interpreted his remark to mean that I should move my parents, brothers, and little sister away from the front of the line. And so we went all the way to the back and therefore missed the first transport out, a shipment of 2,400 Jews who went straight to the gas chambers. There were no selections, no survivors.

Only my intuition in interpreting my relative's remarks about not going to a wedding had enabled me to survive to see my own wedding.

I was among the 152 Siemiatycze Jews selected for the slower death of slave labor in Treblinka I rather than the gas chambers and ashes of Treblinka II. It was dizzying to think of being married after what I had been through.

Without a Jewish community, a synagogue, or a rabbi, the logistics of a wedding seemed absurd. But my future father-in-law felt that we should not have to wait for circumstances to change. From the joyous moment that he confirmed that we wanted to be married, he set about planning the wedding. He found a survivor rabbi, together with a minyan of ten Jews, in the city of Częstochowa. We moved there and were married on May 1, 1945. That Tuesday the Germans formally surrendered to Soviet, American, and British forces. Our wedding day also coincided with Lag B'omer.*

The rabbi who performed our wedding, the first in Częstochowa after the war, had a long, full beard. As he chanted the blessings under the *chuppa* (wedding canopy), I wondered by what miracle this man could have survived a concentration camp with this beard. My eyes began to wander to the assembled guests, searching for familiar faces. Where were my parents, my sister, and my brothers at a time like this? My vision blurred and I suddenly saw them all smiling beside me near the wedding canopy. I screamed out, "Mamma! Pappa!" and lost my balance.

My in-laws told me that I had fainted. The emotional strain was too much. I recovered and went on with the ceremony. There was great comfort in the familiarity of the rituals. They gave me faith that there was still a world where the Creator of men and women was busy making matches.

I was proud of my father-in-law's rocklike faith. He never failed to pray three times a day—before, during, and after the war. During the war he had even refrained from eating *hametz* (leavened products) during the week of Passover. This meant living on potatoes alone, without any of the old bread that normally kept us all going.

With no quorum of worshipers and no synagogue, my pious father-in-law made his morning, afternoon, and evening prayers alone, deep within his underground bunker. Surely he must have repeated, as I

*See the note on p. 78.

often had, the verse from Psalms: "From the depths I call to Thee O' Lord." He found enough joy somehow to continue singing the Sabbath *zmiros*.* Truly he had sustained his hungry family on this banquet of faith.

Forced to work on the Sabbath in Treblinka, I renewed my observance of the Sabbath after I escaped. I remained completely faithful and never forgot that the Bible promises great punishments as well as great rewards for the eternal people of Israel. Never did I dream at that time that my people would re-establish our homeland in Palestine in my lifetime. The miracle of the state of Israel only confirmed my belief that the historic events of my generation were as monumental as the Jews' redemption from Egyptian slavery, the destruction of the Temple in Jerusalem, and the flowering of rabbinic Judaism in Babylonia.

* *Zmiros* are Hebrew hymns traditionally sung at Sabbath meals.

Shadows of Treblinka

*A*fter the war, memories often resurfaced in sweat-soaked nightmares. Many of these concerned all the little incidents that together led to my miraculous survival. The unselfishness of Siemiatycze townsmen like Meyer Pinchesowitz and Lonchik the accountant helped to save my life. They had once had a good opportunity to escape but had decided not to try. They knew that the remaining seventy Jews of their town would be killed in retaliation, so they did not run with the rest of their outside work detail when the Ukrainian guard fell asleep. Instead, they waited for the guard to wake up and pointed the pursuing Germans in the wrong direction. None of the escapees were caught, and no one was executed in revenge. Because of their nobility I was able to live. These two great souls were among the 5,000 holy martyrs of Siemiatycze who perished in Treblinka. Whenever I think of the miracle of my life I bow to these men with a prayer to G-d on my lips.

Only two Jews from our town survived Treblinka I—Binyamin Rock and me, Saul Kuperhand. After the war Rock emigrated to Palestine. Before he left he too made it back to Siemiatycze, where I heard his story of survival. As the war was ending the Nazis shot every last inmate, even their loyal friends the *kapos*. These supermen did not want to leave any witnesses to their barbaric crimes. Benjamin Rock was also shot, but he managed to crawl into the well near the kitchen. A carpenter, he had prepared a long thin ladder to drop into the well in just such a situation. Wounded and exhausted, he and a handful of other men managed to hold on to that ladder in the blackness of the well for days until they finally heard the voices of Russian soldiers.

As they helped the men climb out of the well the Russians could not believe that Jewish inmates had managed to cling to life in such circumstances. I remembered the well about which he spoke. I associated it with death, not life, because many starved and depressed inmates had jumped into it head-first to end their terrible suffering.

Binyamin Rock discovered what had happened to the rest of the Jewish prisoners who had survived until the Russian advance. Marched to some specially prepared ditches in a nearby forest, they had all been shot. With very few exceptions the Jews who entered Treblinka perished.

At my father-in-law's informal center for survivors I also spent time with Carl Carson and Izac Helfinger. I do not know how the three of us made it through, but we all eventually ended up in America. Carl married a lovely woman named Paula and opened a butcher shop. We spent some time with them in Michigan where they lived with three children and two grandchildren. Later, unfortunately, Carl became ill with cancer. We visited him when he was in Boston for treatment, and, toward the end of his life, we went to see him in Fort Lauderdale, Florida. Losing Carl was like losing a brother and a best friend. After what we went through together, we survivors from the Siemiatycze area were closer than family.

I will never forget how, despite his illness, Carl traveled to my son David's wedding. He told me that my happiness was his and that nothing could stop him from celebrating this great occasion with me and the other survivors from our town. I offered a toast in his honor, reminding the assembled guests that the wedding might never have taken place if it had not been for Carl's courage and generosity. I sometimes view the videotape made of the wedding in order to see him and our precious fellow survivors smiling together. After Carl passed away we remained close to his wife and his youngest daughter, Phyllis. As a Manhattanite, Phyllis often visits my own daughter's store in New York or her home in Teaneck, New Jersey. She stays in touch with all of us by phone.

We survivors are a small and shrinking community. It is hard to explain how important these contacts are for us. Despite the anxiety he caused us in the bunker, I even wanted to make contact with Izac Helfinger. I had lost touch with him shortly after he visited my father-in-law's house in Siemiatycze, and I searched for him for thirty years. I finally located him in Beverly Hills, California. We were excited and overjoyed to rediscover each other. When he and his wife, Lola, accepted my invitation to visit us in Brooklyn, I gathered many of our former townsmen to greet him. We celebrated our new lives with a week of visiting and sightseeing with my children and grandchildren. Izac later lost his wife, but he still lives with his two sons in California.

When I consider my adopted siblings, my fellow survivors, I often think with great sadness about my beloved sister, Sarale, who perished in the gas chambers of Treblinka. This memoir is a tribute to all those I lost.

SUGGESTED READINGS

Dobroszycki, Lucjan, and Barbara Kirshenblatt-Gimblett. *Image before My Eyes: A Photographic History of Jewish Life in Poland, 1864–1939*. New York: Schocken, 1977.

Gutman, Yisrael, Ezra Mendelsohn, Jehuda Reinharz, and Chone Shmeruk, eds. *The Jews of Poland between the Two World Wars*. Hanover, N.H.: University Press of New England, 1989.

Heller, Celia Stopnicka. *On the Edge of Destruction: The Jews of Poland between the Two World Wars*. New York: Columbia University Press, 1977.

Kugelmass, Jack, and Jonathan Boyarin. *From a Ruined Garden: The Memorial Books of Polish Jewry*. New York: Schocken, 1983.

Mendelsohn, Ezra. *The Jews of East Central Europe between the World Wars.* Bloomington: Indiana University Press, 1983.

———. *On Modern Jewish Politics*. New York: Oxford University Press, 1993.

Sierakowiak, Dawid. *The Diary of Dawid Sierakowiak*, ed. Alan Adelson. New York: Oxford University Press, 1996.

Tash (Tur-Shalom), Eliezer, ed. *Kehilat Semyatitsh* (The Community of Semiatych). Tel Aviv: Association of Former Residents of Semiatych in Israel and the Diaspora, 1965. A copy of this publication is available in the library of the Institute for Jewish Research, New York, N.Y.

Yoran, Shalom. *The Defiant*. New York: St. Martin's Press, 1996.

Zuckerman, Yitzchak. *A Surplus of Memory: A Chronicle of the Warsaw Ghetto Uprising*. Edited and translated by Barbara Harshav. Berkeley: University of California Press, 1992.

INDEX

MIRIAM KUPERHAND (née Grodzicki) was born in Kałuszyn, Poland, in 1926. She and her family survived the Nazi liquidation of the Siemiatyzce Ghetto in November 1942 and spent the remainder of the war living under subhuman conditions in the Polish countryside. SAUL KUPERHAND was born in Siemiatyzce in 1922. He and his family were part of the final deportation from Siemiatyzce to the notorious Treblinka death camp, from which he managed to escape in September 1943. The Kuperhands were married on May 1, 1945, in Częstochowa, Poland, and eventually moved to Paris with their three children. They came to the United States in 1959, settling first in Newark, New Jersey, and later in Brooklyn, New York. Now retired from their family clothing business, they live in Boca Raton, Florida.

ALAN ADELSON is the executive director of the Jewish Heritage Project in New York. He produced and, with Kathryn Taverna, directed the acclaimed documentary film *Łódź Ghetto*, compiled and edited its widely used companion volume, *Łódź Ghetto: Inside a Community under Siege*, and has prepared and brought to publication many works of literature from the Holocaust, including most recently *The Diary of Dawid Sierakowiak*.